CGP

Mireille Hagan

Non-Verbal Reasoning

The 11+ Practice Book

with Assessment Tests

For GL & other test providers

Ages

8-9

Practise • Prepare • Pass

Everything your child needs for 11+ success

How to use this Practice Book

This book is divided into two parts — Spotting Patterns and Assessment Tests.
There are answers and detailed explanations in the pull-out section at the back of the book.

Spotting Patterns

- Each section contains practice questions focusing on one of the main concepts your child will need to understand for the Non-Verbal Reasoning test.
- These pages can help your child build up the different skills they'll need for the real test.

Assessment Tests

- The second half of the book contains ten assessment tests, each with a mix of question types. They're similar to the real test.
- You can print off multiple-choice answer sheets from our website, www.cgplearning.co.uk/11+, so your child can practise taking the tests as if they're sitting the real thing.
- If you want to give your child timed practice, set a time limit of 15 minutes for each test, and ask them to work as quickly and carefully as they can.
- The tests get harder from 1-10, so don't be surprised if your child finds the later ones more tricky.
- Talk your child through the answers to any questions they got wrong. This will help them understand questions that work in a similar way when they come up against them in later tests.
- Your child should aim for a mark of around 85% (24 questions correct) in each test. If they score less than this, use their results to work out the areas they need more practice on.
- If they haven't managed to finish the test on time, they need to work on increasing their speed, whereas if they have made a lot of mistakes, they need to work more carefully.
- Keep track of your child's scores using the progress chart on the inside back cover of the book.

Published by CGP

Editors:
Ceara Hayden, Sharon Keeley-Holden, Anthony Muller and Rebecca Tate

With thanks to Claire Boulter and Alexandra Reynolds for the proofreading.

ISBN: 978 1 84762 833 6
Printed by Elanders Ltd, Newcastle upon Tyne
Clipart from Corel®

Based on the classic CGP style created by Richard Parsons.

CONTENTS

Spotting Patterns

Assessment Tests

Shapes

Looking at the shapes in a question is often a good place to start.

Warm Up

1. How many **sides** does each shape have?

a. b. c. d. e. f.

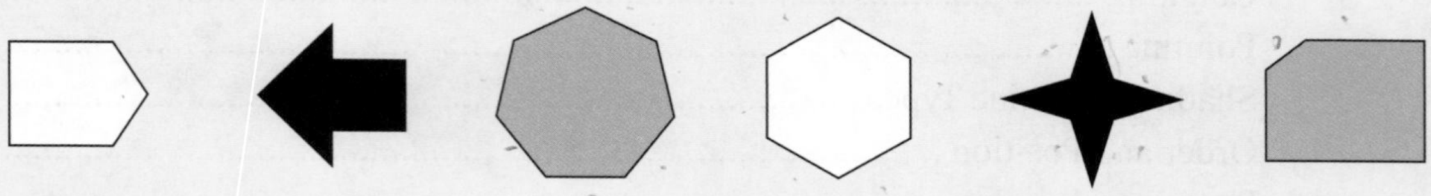

5   7   7   6   8   5

2. How many of the **grey shapes** on the right have the **same number** of **sides** as the grey shape inside the square?

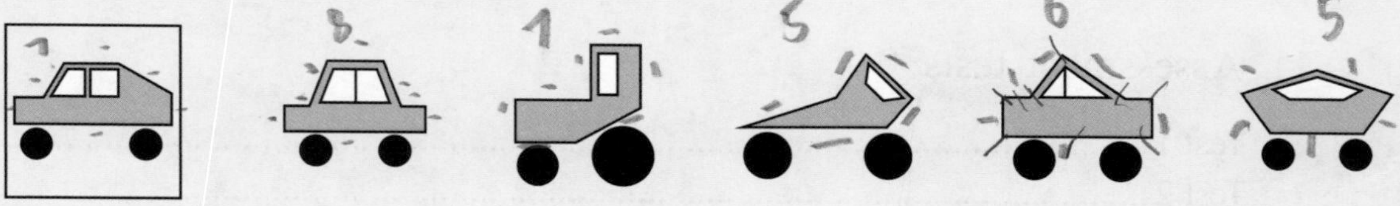

Number of **same-sided** grey shapes: 1

Find the Figure Like the First Two

Work out which of the figures on the right is most like the two figures on the left.

Example:

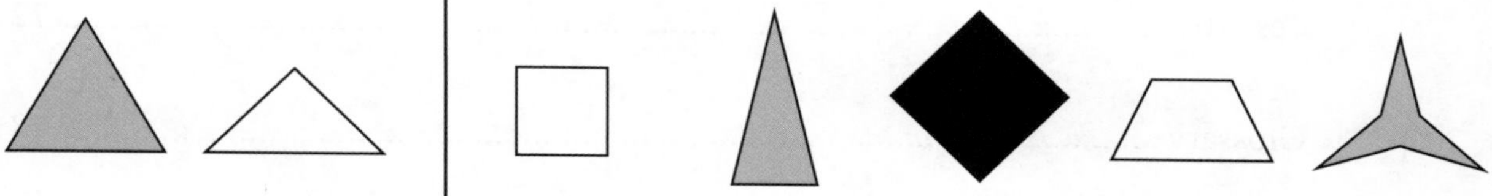

a b c d e

All figures must have three sides. (b)

3.

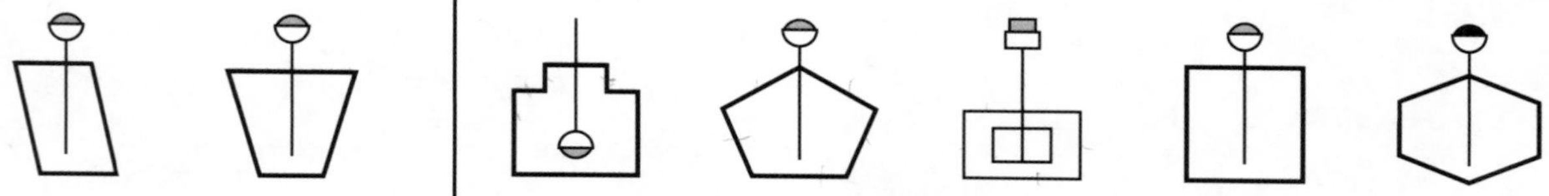

a b c d e

( )

4.

a b c d e

( )

5.

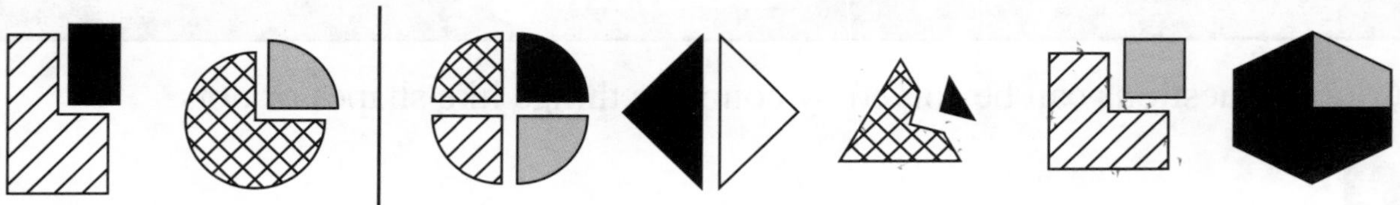

a b c d e

( )

Vertical Code

Each question has three figures on the left with code letters that describe them. You need to work out what the code letters mean. The figure on the right is missing its code. Work out which of the five codes on the right describes this figure.

Example:

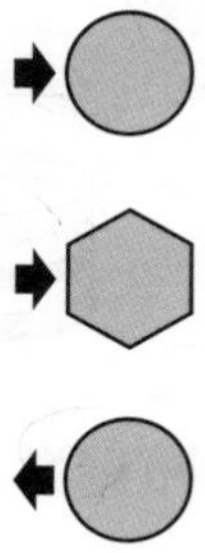

S

T

S

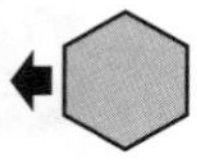

T	Q	R	S	P
a	b	c	d	e

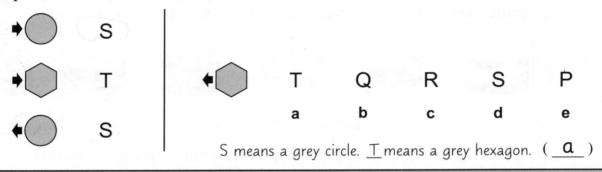

S means a grey circle. T means a grey hexagon. (a)

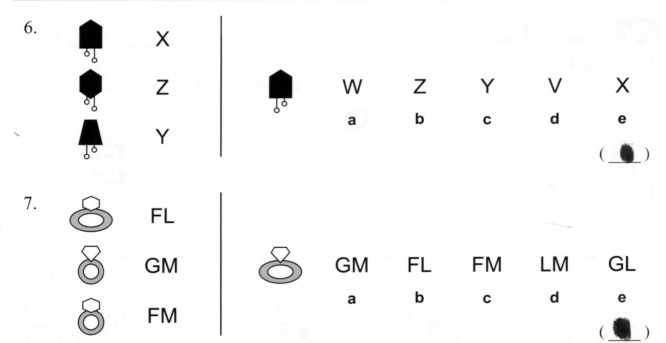

6.

X

Z

Y

W	Z	Y	V	X
a	b	c	d	e

( )

7.

FL

GM

FM

GM	FL	FM	LM	GL
a	b	c	d	e

( )

8.

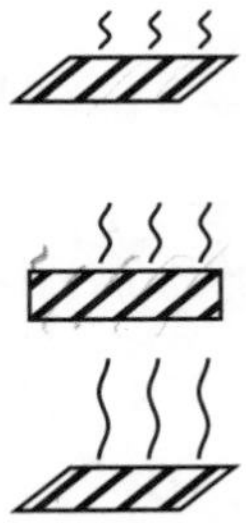

CP

BQ

DP

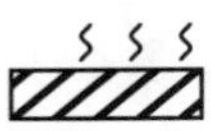

BP	CQ	CP	DQ	DP
a	b	c	d	e

( )

Counting

A lot of questions can be solved by counting things like shapes or dots.

Warm Up

1. How many **circles** are there in each figure?

a. b. c. d. e. f.

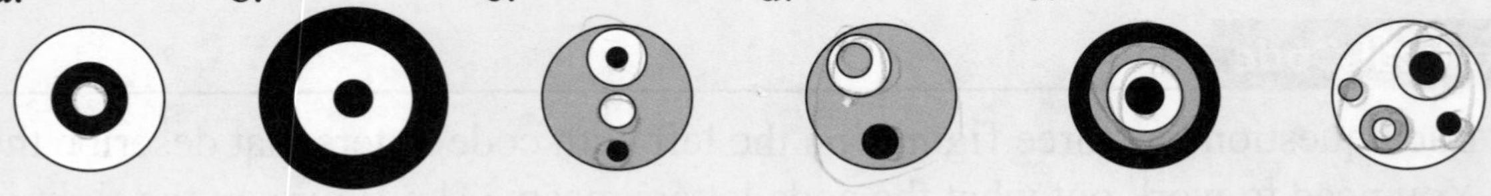

3 3 5 4 4 7

2. How many of these cakes have the **same** number of **layers** as the one inside the square? How many have the **same** number of **cherries**?

Number of cakes with the **same number** of **layers**: 2

Number of cakes with the **same number** of **cherries**: 1

Complete the Series

The squares on the left are arranged in order. One of the squares is empty. Work out which of the squares on the right should replace the empty square.

Example:

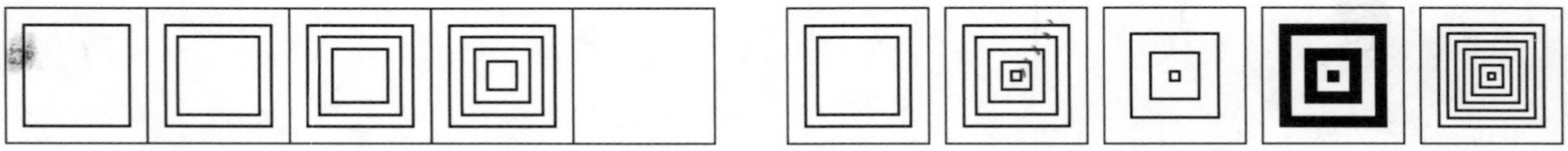

a b c d e

An extra square is added in each series square. (b)

3.

a b c d e

( )

4.

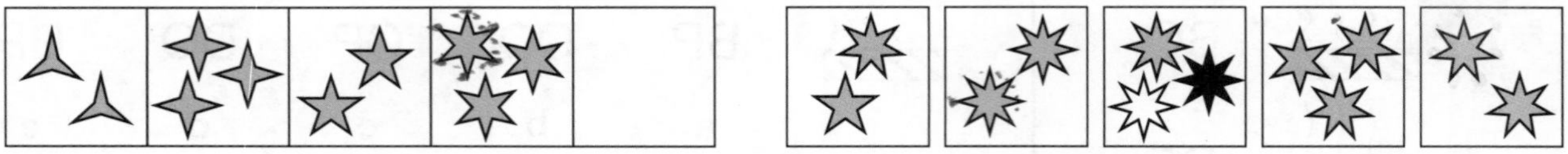

a b c d e

( )

5.

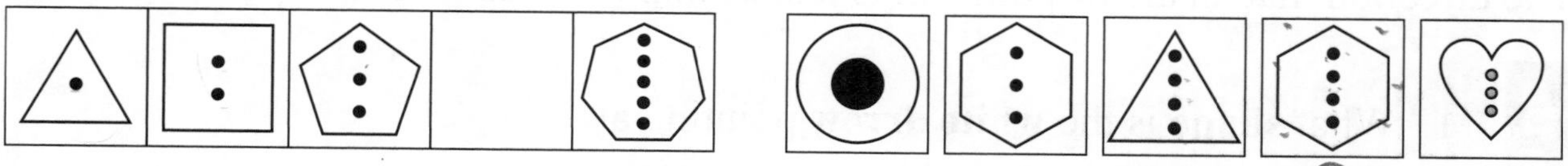

a b c d e

(___)

Find the Figure Like the First Three

Find the figure on the right that is most like the three figures on the left.

Example:

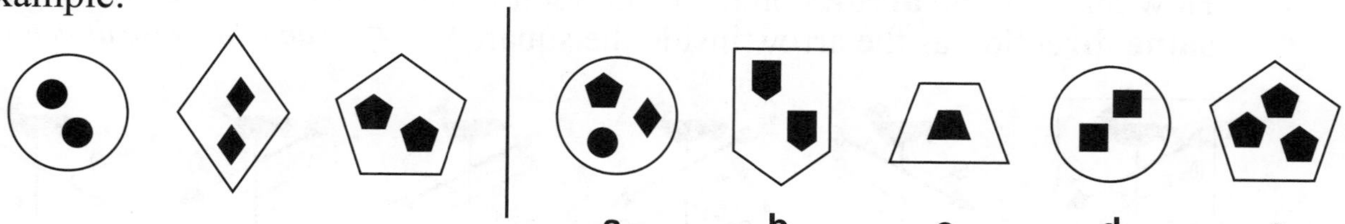

a b c d e

All figures must have two inner shapes that are identical to the outer shape apart from size and shading. (b)

6.

a b c d e

(___)

7.

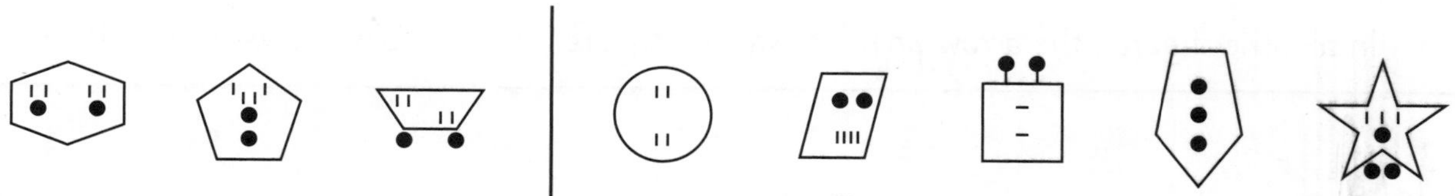

a b c d e

(___)

8.

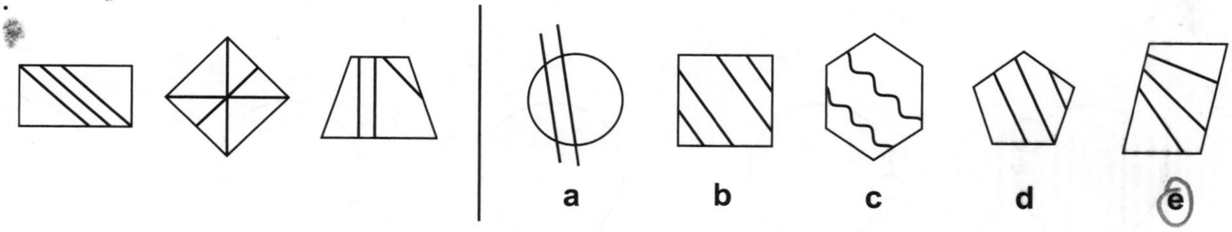

a b c d e

(___)

Pointing

The direction that an arrow points in is just as important as what it is pointing at.

Warm Up

1. What **shape** is the **white arrow** pointing at?

a. b. c. d. e. f.

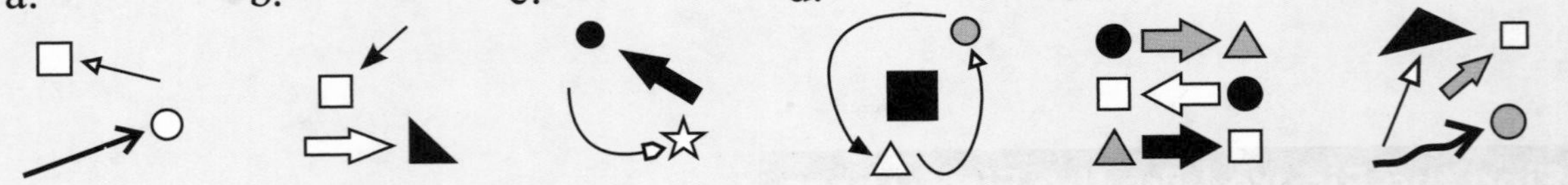

square | triangle | circle | circle | square | triangle

2. How many of the **arrows** on the right point in the **same direction** as the arrow inside the square?

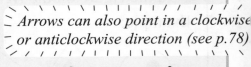

Arrows can also point in a clockwise or anticlockwise direction (see p.78).

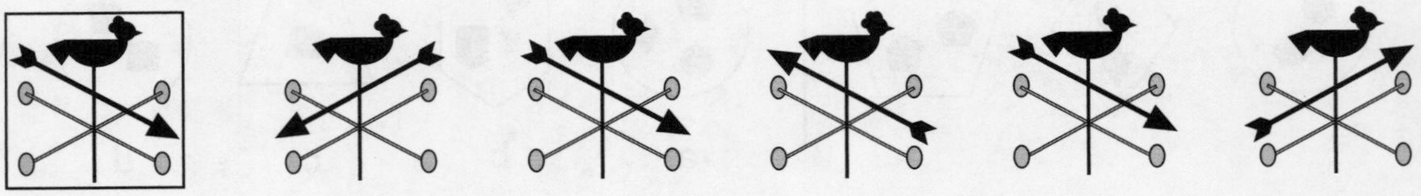

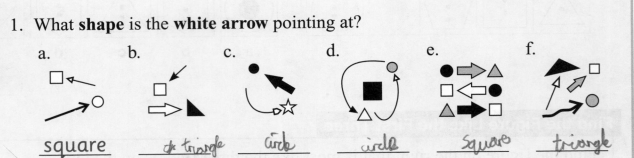

Number of **arrows** that point in the **same direction**: 2

Odd One Out

Look at the five figures below. Find the figure that is most unlike the others.

Example:

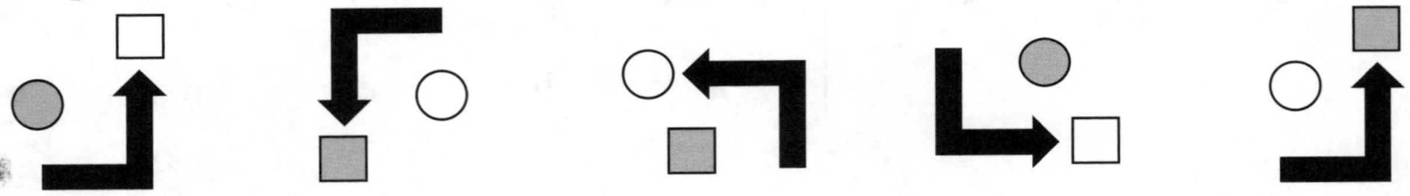

a b c d e

In all other figures, the arrow points towards a square. In C it points towards a circle. (C)

3.

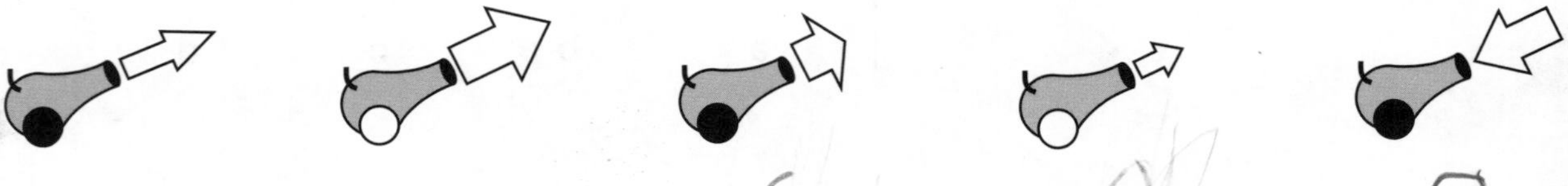

a b c d e

([redacted])

4.

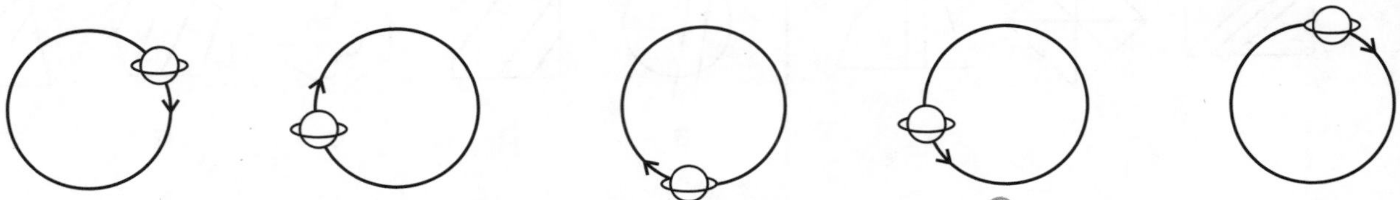

a b c d e

([redacted])

5.

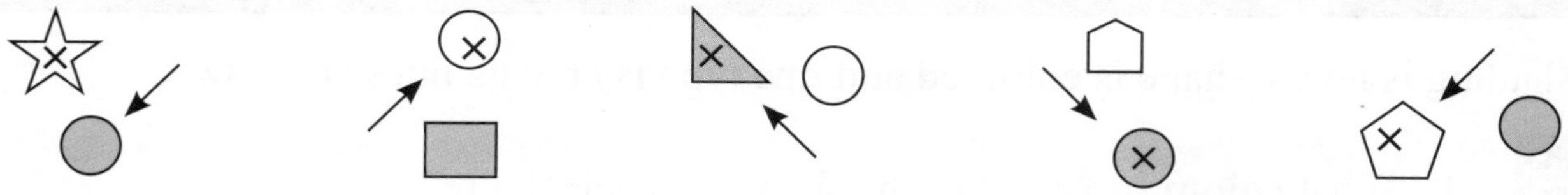

a b c d e

(____)

Find the Figure Like the First Two

Find the figure on the right that is most like the two figures on the left.

Example:

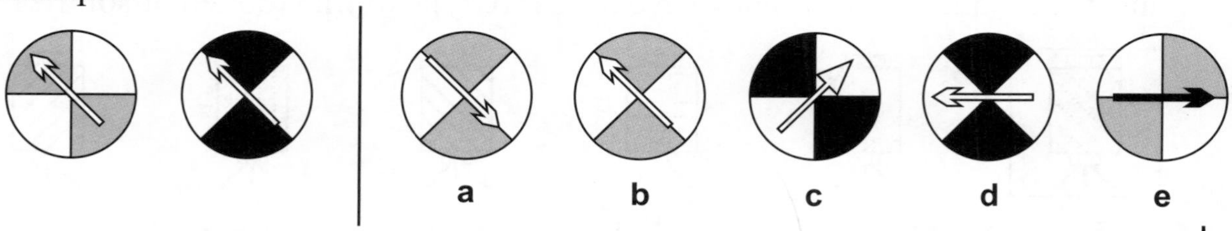

a b c d e

In all figures, the arrow must point towards the top left. (b)

6.

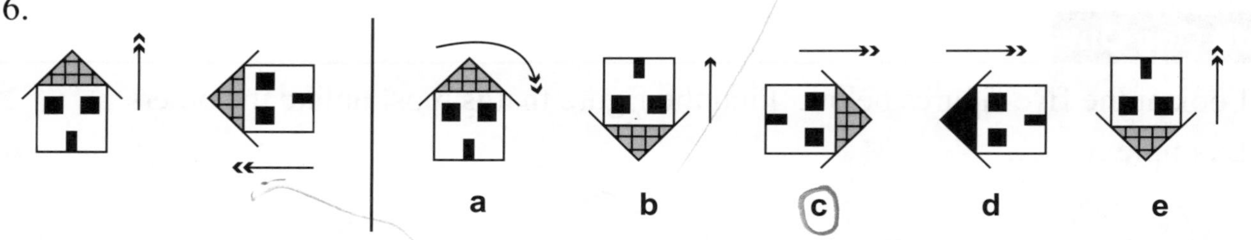

a b c d e

(____)

7.

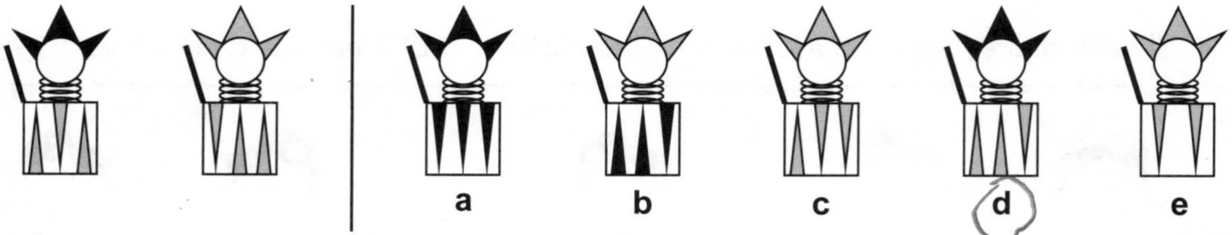

a b c d e

(____)

8.

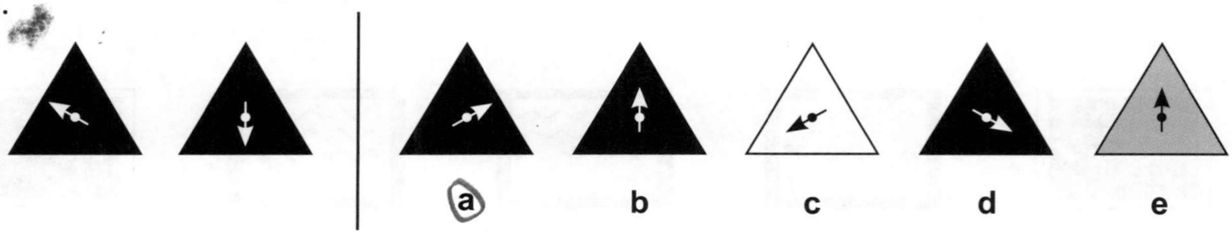

a b c d e

(____)

Shading and Line Types

Shading is how a shape is coloured and line type is how its lines are drawn.

Warm Up

1. What **colour** are **most** of the shapes in each figure?

a. b. c. d. e. f.

grey ___ ___ ___ ___ ___

2. How many paintings have the **same direction** of **hatching** as the painting inside the square? How many have the **same type** of **line** (dotted or solid)?

Number of paintings with the **same direction** of **hatching**: ___

Number of paintings with the **same type** of **line**: ___

Odd One Out

Look at the five figures below. Find the figure that is most unlike the others.

Example:

a b c d e

In all other figures, the big shape has a dashed outline. In D it has a dotted outline. (d)

3.

a b c d e

([redacted])

4.

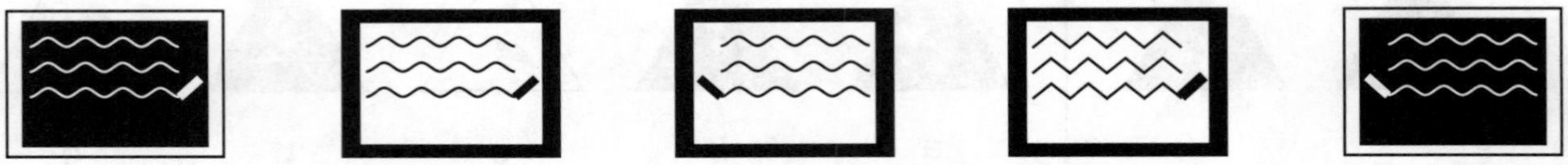

a b c d e

([redacted])

5.

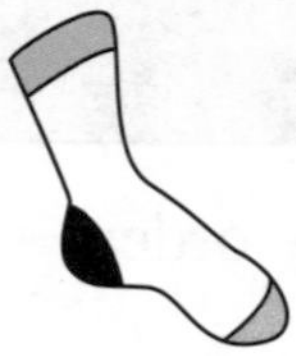 a

 b

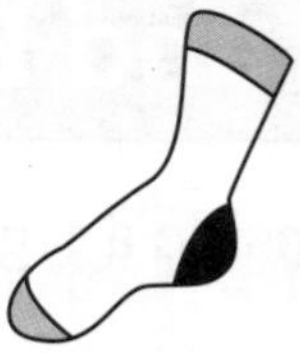 c

 d

 e

([redacted])

Vertical Code

Each question has three figures on the left with code letters that describe them. You need to work out what the code letters mean. The figure on the right is missing its code. Work out which of the five codes on the right describes this figure.

Example:

 G

 F

 G

H	G	K	F	J
a	b	c	d	e

F means the shapes are white, G means they are black. (d)

6.

 S

 R

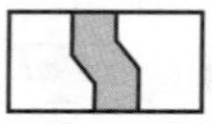 T

S	Q	R	T	P
a	b	c	d	e

([redacted])

7.

 LR

 MS

 MR

MS	LR	LS	MR	LM
a	b	c	d	e

([redacted])

8.

 DX

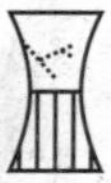 DZ

 CY

CZ	DX	DZ	DY	CX
a	b	c	d	e

([redacted])

Order and Position

Shapes can be in different positions inside a figure. They can also change order.

Warm Up

1. Which shape is **one place clockwise** from the **circle** in each figure?

a. b. c. d. e.

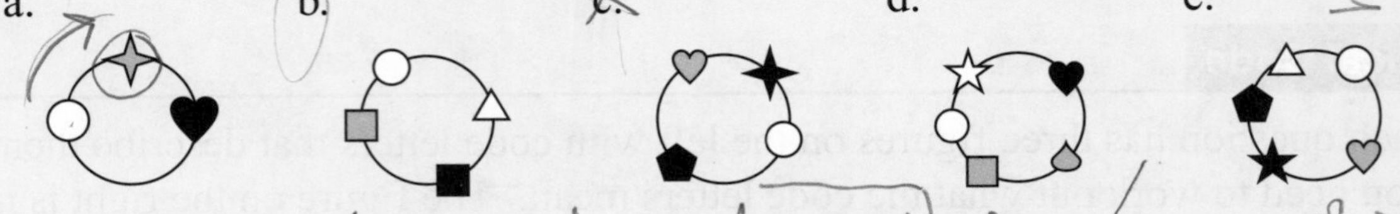

a. star

2. How many figures on the right have the **same order** of **shapes** going from top to bottom as the figure inside the square (ignoring size)?

Number of figures with the **same order** of **shapes**: ____

Find the Figure Like the First Three

Work out which of the figures on the right is most like the three figures on the left.

Example:

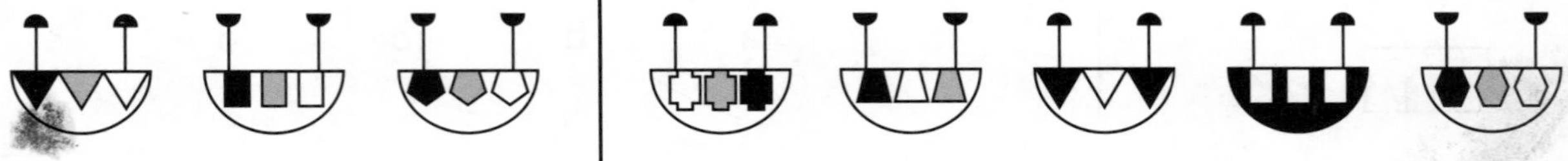

a b c d e

In all figures, the three inner shapes go from left to right in the order: black, grey, white. (e)

3.

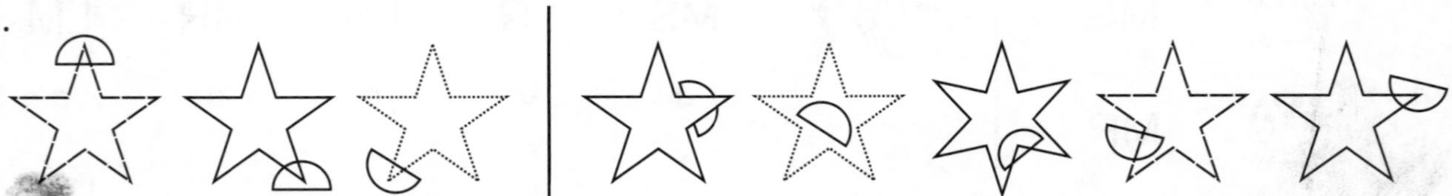

a b c d e

(____)

4.

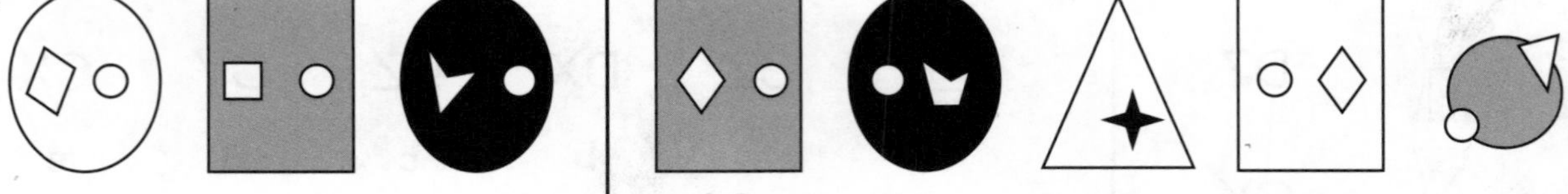

a b c d e

(____)

5.

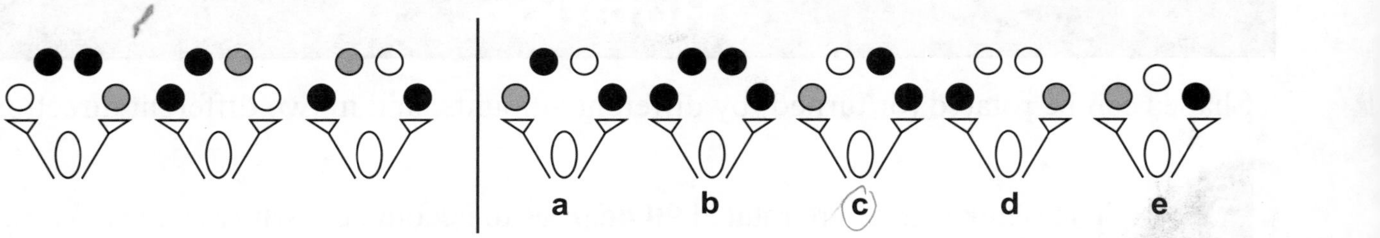

a b c d e

([redacted])

Complete the Pair

The first figure in each question changes to become the second figure. Work out how the first figure has been changed. Then find the figure on the right that would match the third figure if it was changed in the same way.

Example:

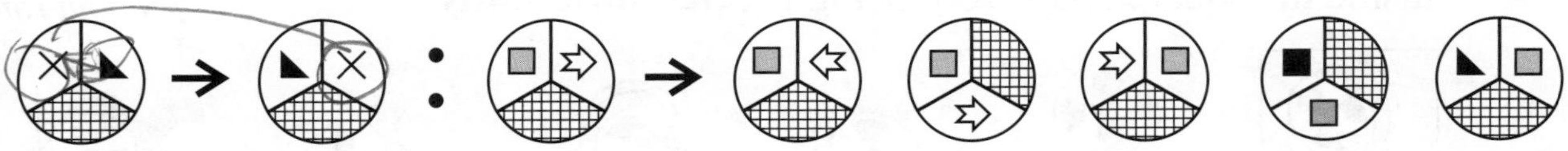

a b c d e

The top left hand shape and the top right hand shape swap places. (C)

6.

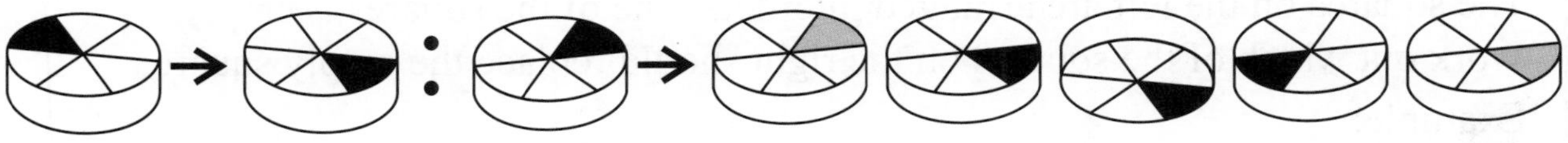

a b c d e

([redacted])

7.

a b c d e

([redacted])

8.

a b c d e

([redacted])

Rotation

Shapes can be rotated (or turned) by different amounts, and in two different directions.

Warm Up

1. The **black** shapes are rotated **90 degrees** to become the **white** shapes. Work out which **direction** they are rotated. Write **C** for clockwise or **A** for anticlockwise.

a. b. c. d. e. f.

a. C b. ____ c. ____ d. ____ e. ____ f. ____

2. How many figures on the right are **identical** to the figure inside the square apart from being **rotated differently**?

See p.78 for more about rotation.

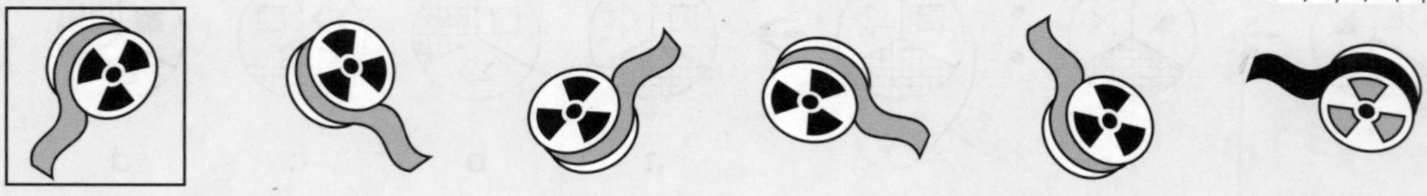

Number of **identical figures:** ____

Complete the Series

The squares on the left are arranged in order. One of the squares is empty. Work out which of the squares on the right should replace the empty square.

Example:

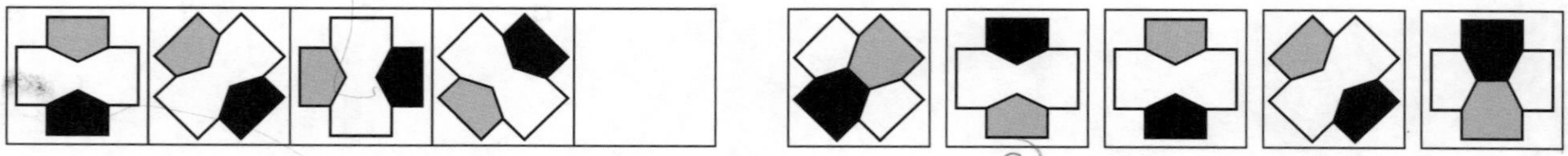

a b c d e

The figure rotates 45 degrees anticlockwise in each series square. (b)

3.

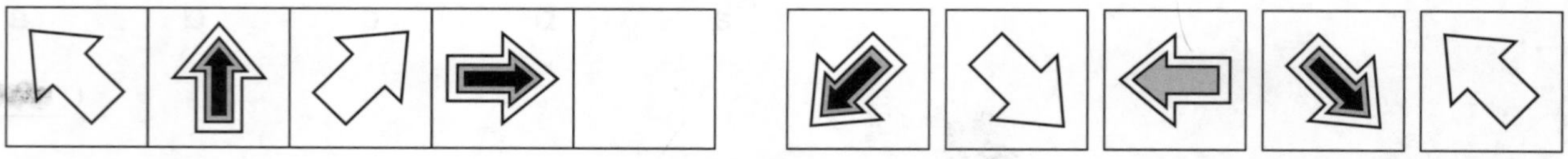

a b c d e

(____)

4.

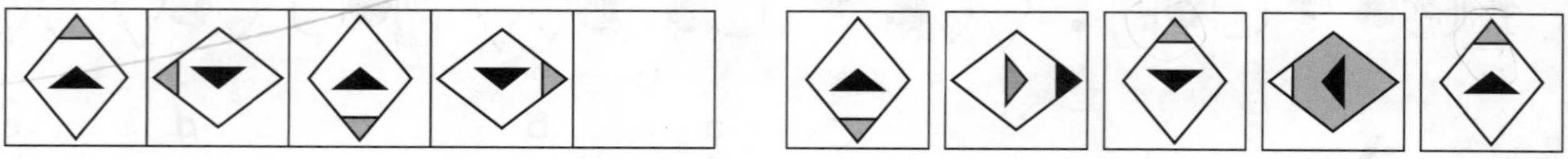

a b c d e

(____)

5.

a b c d e

([redacted])

Complete the Grid

On the left of each question below is a grid with one empty square.
Work out which of the five squares on the right should replace the empty square.

Example:

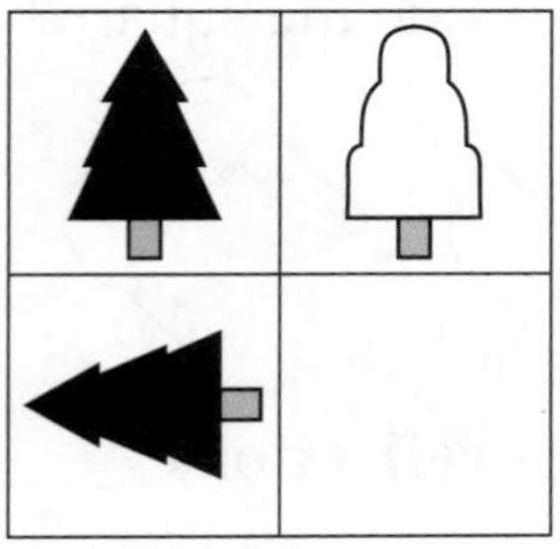

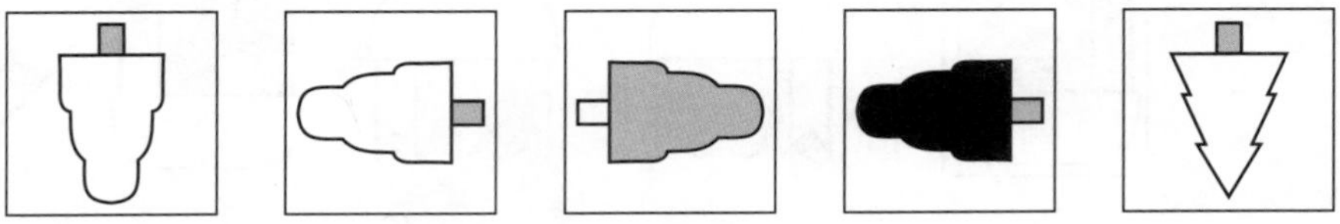

a b c d e

Working from top to bottom, the figure rotates 90 degrees anticlockwise. (b)

6.

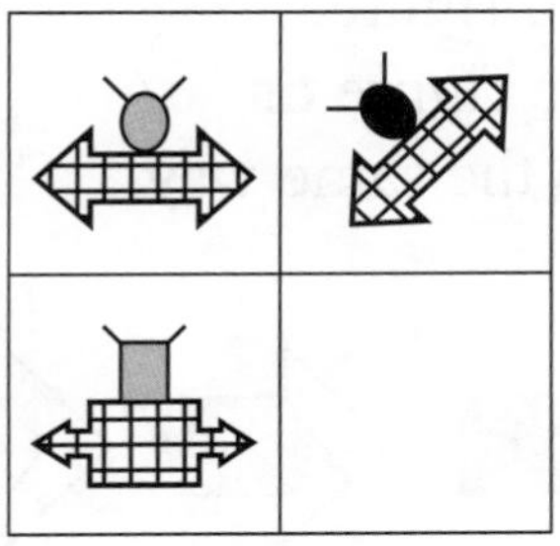

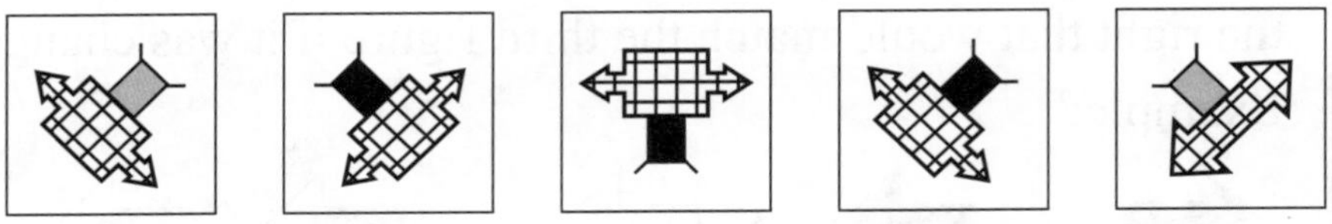

a b c d e

([redacted])

7.

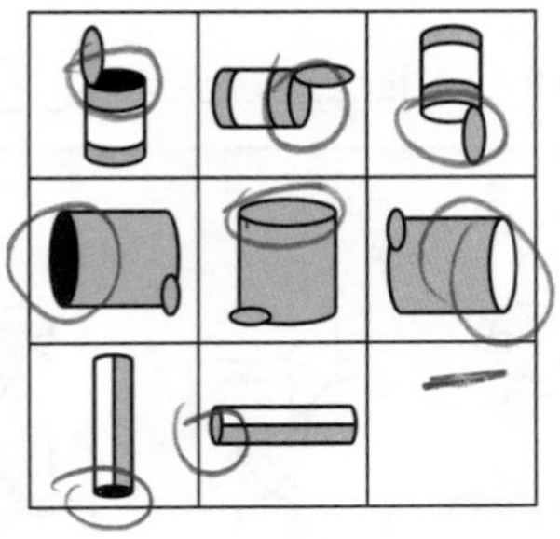

a b c d e

([redacted])

8.

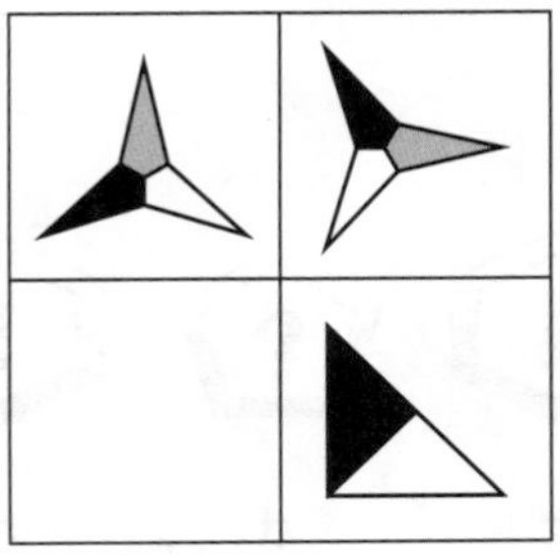

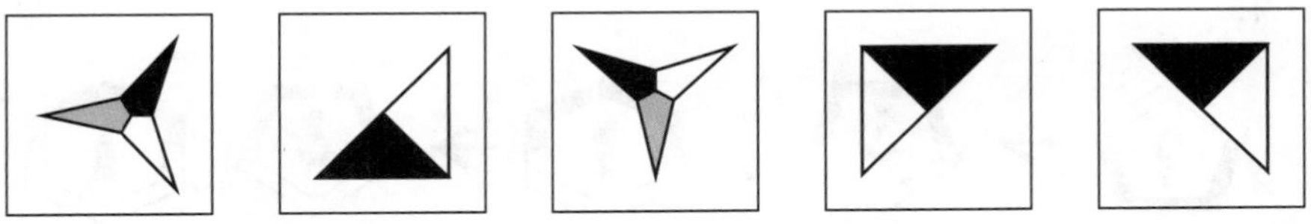

a b c d e

([redacted])

Reflection

The reflection of a shape is how it would look in a mirror.

Warm Up

1. Is the black shape a **sideways reflection** of the white shape? Write **yes** or **no**.

a. b. c. d. e. f.

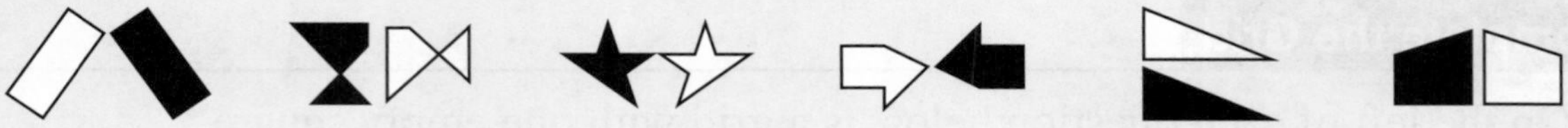

a. yes b. No c. Yes d. NO e. Yes f. Yes

2. How many of these figures are **reflections** of the figure inside the square?

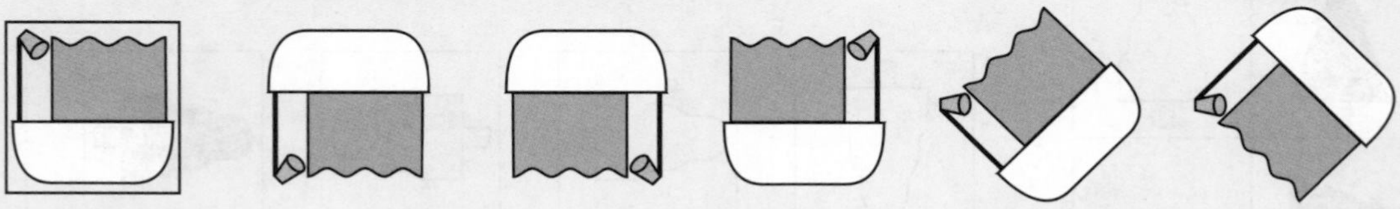

Number of **reflections**: 1

Complete the Pair

The first figure in each question changes to become the second figure. Work out how the first figure has been changed. Then find the figure on the right that would match the third figure if it was changed in the same way.

Example:

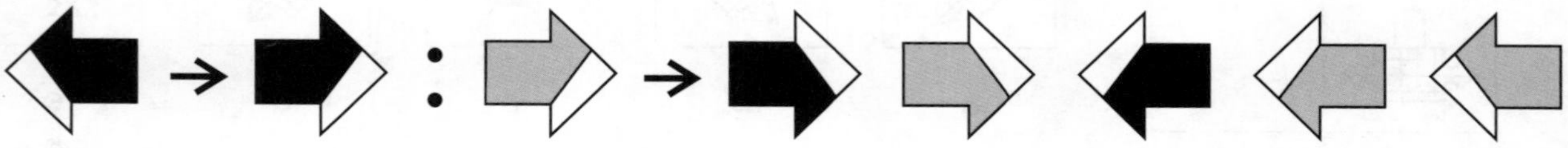

a b c d e

The figure reflects across. (e)

3.

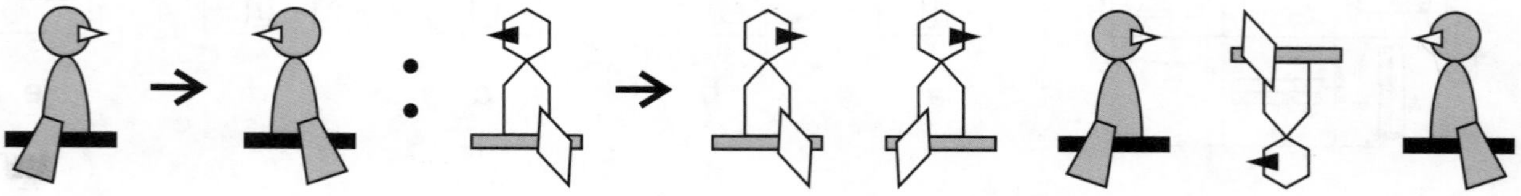

a b c d e

(B)

4.

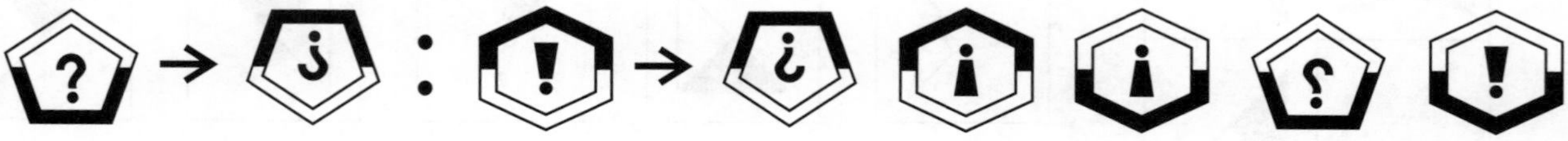

a b c d e

(C)

5.

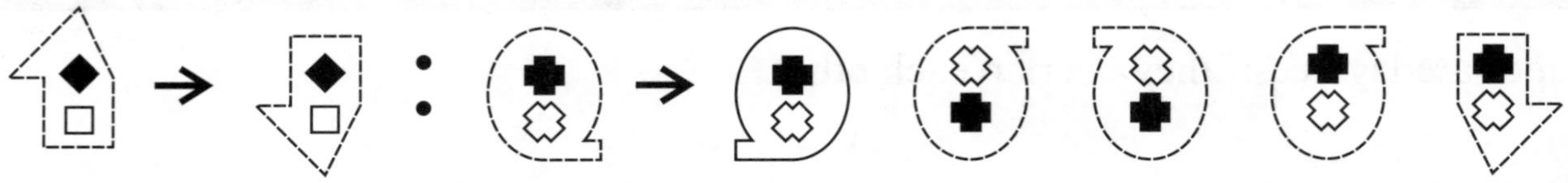

a b c d e

(B)

Complete the Grid

On the left of each question below is a grid with one empty square.
Work out which of the five squares on the right should replace the empty square.

Example:

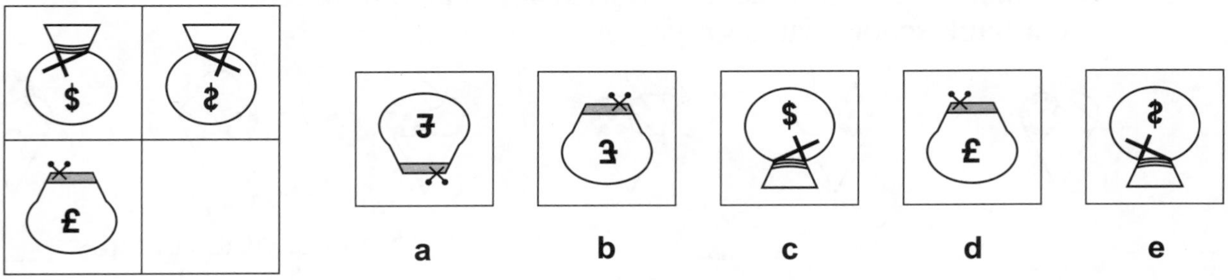

a b c d e

Working from left to right, the figure reflects across. (b)

6.

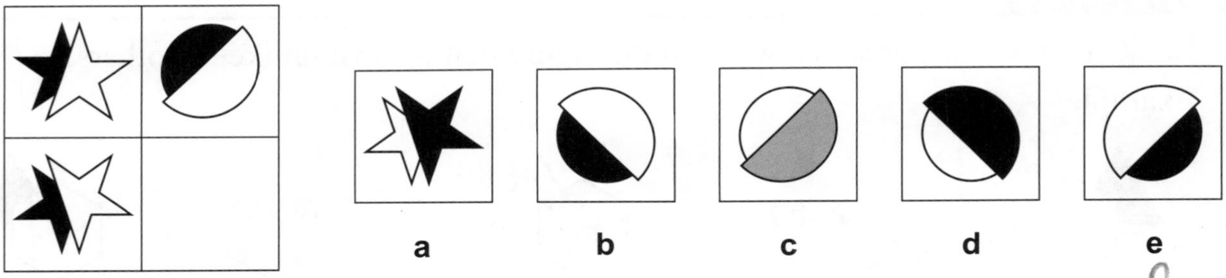

a b c d e

(B)

7.

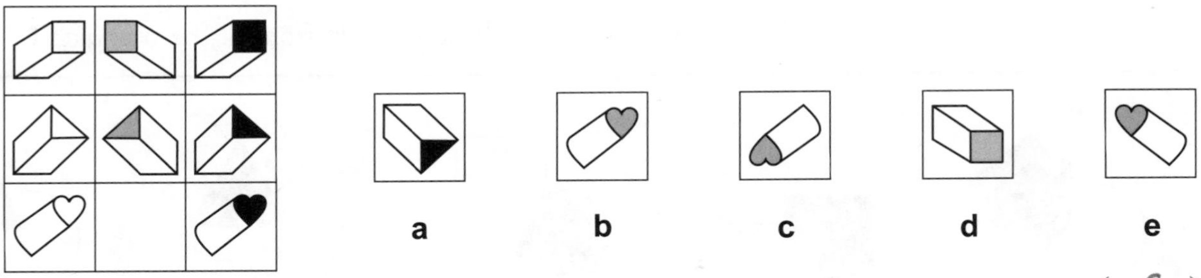

a b c d e

(e)

8.

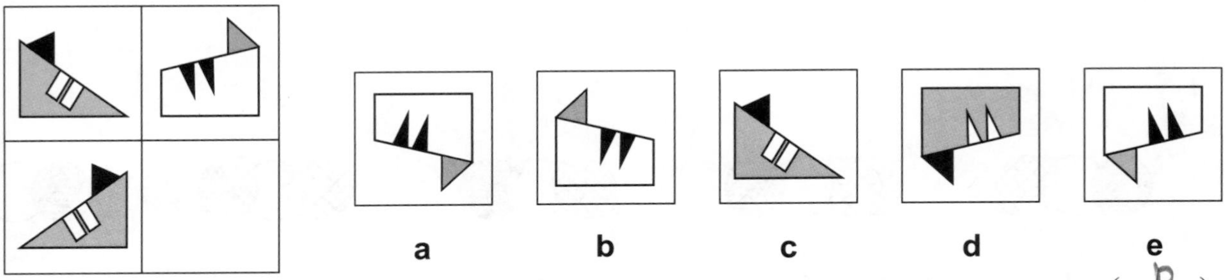

a b c d e

(B)

Layering

Shapes are layered if they overlap each other.

Warm Up

1. What **shape** is at the **front** of each of the figures below?

a. b. c. d. e. f.

a. circle

2. How many ice creams have a **front scoop** that is **hatched**, and a **back scoop** that is **grey**?

Number of ice creams: ____

Odd One Out

Look at the five figures below. Find the figure that is most unlike the others.

Example:

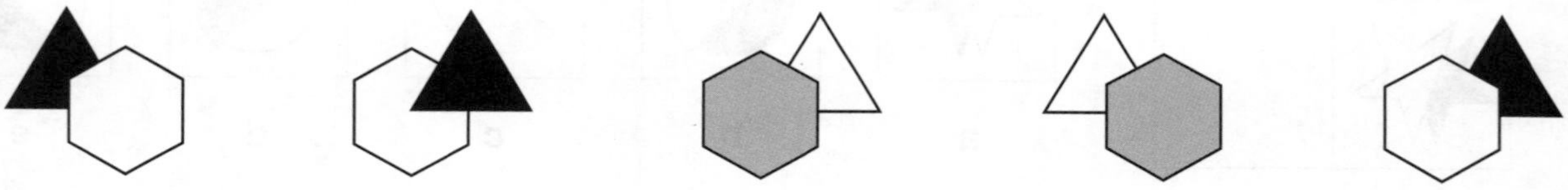

a b c d e

In all other figures, the hexagon is in front of the triangle. (b)

3.

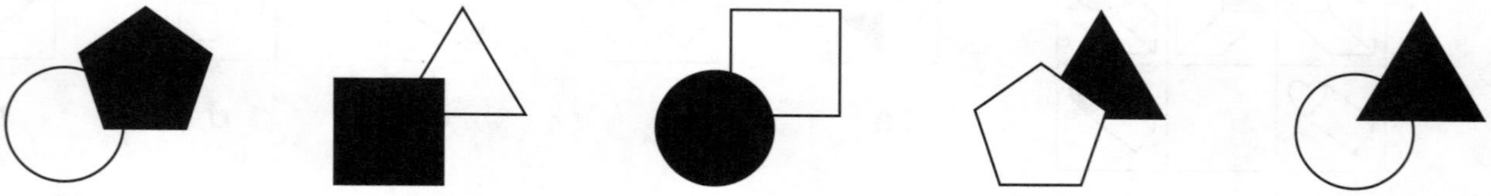

a b c d e

(____)

4.

a b c d e

(____)

5.

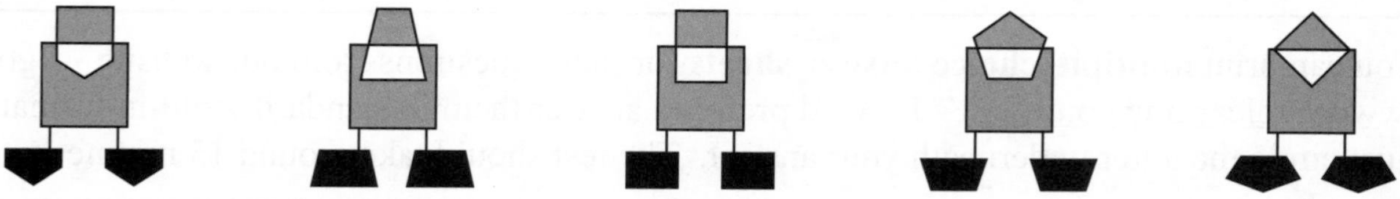

a b c d e

(____)

Complete the Pair

The first figure in each question changes to become the second figure. Work out how the first figure has been changed. Then find the figure on the right that would match the third figure if it was changed in the same way.

Example:

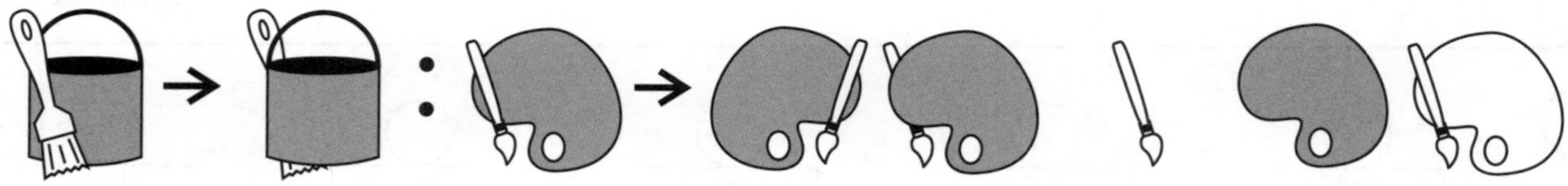

a b c d e

The shape at the front moves to the back. (b)

6.

a b c d e

(____)

7.

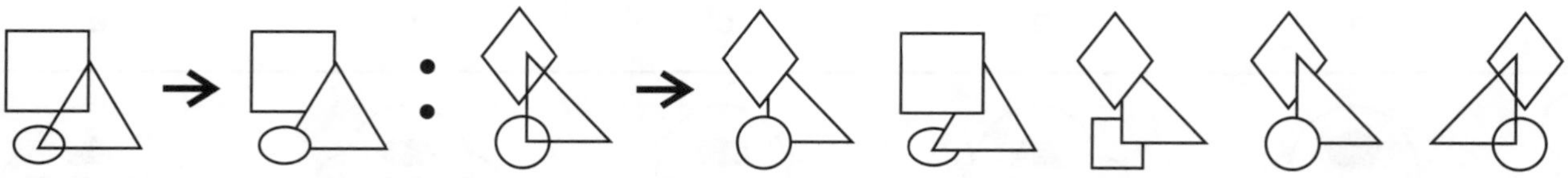

a b c d e

(____)

8.

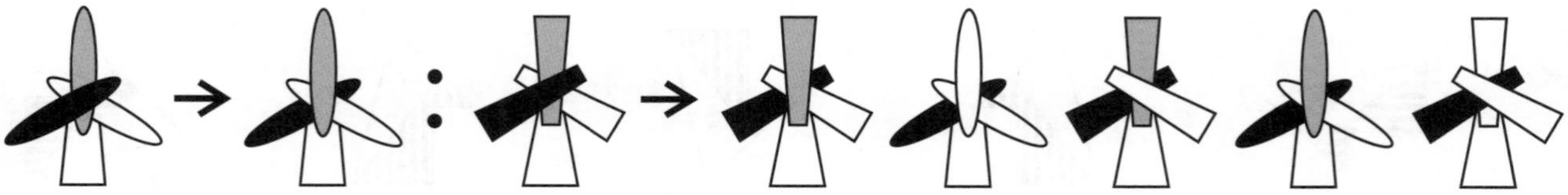

a b c d e

(____)

Assessment Test 1

You can print **multiple-choice answer sheets** for these questions from our website — go to www.cgplearning.co.uk/11+. If you'd prefer to answer them in standard write-in format, just circle the letter underneath your answer. The test should take around 15 minutes.

Section 1 — Odd One Out

Each of the questions below has five figures.
Find the figure in each row that is most unlike the others.

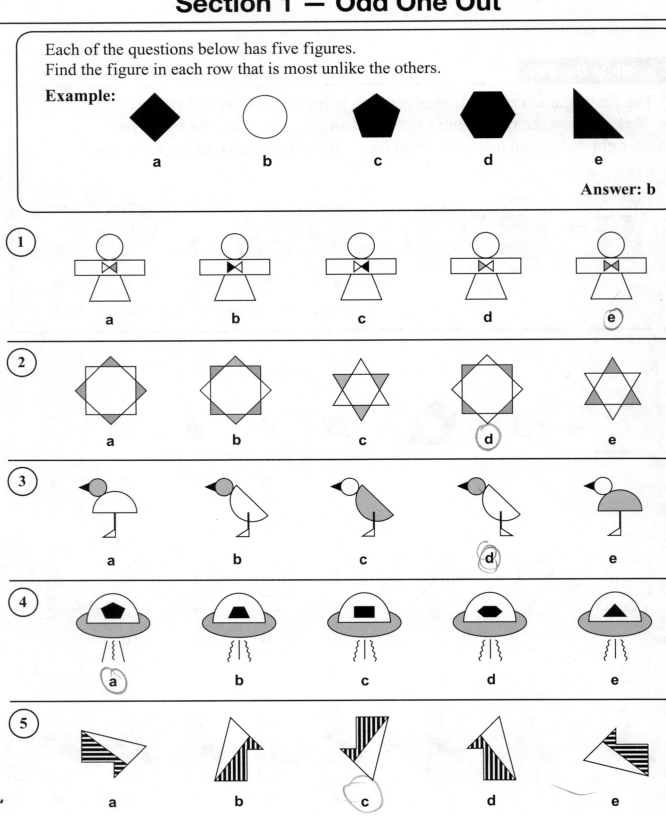

Example:

a b c d e

Answer: b

1

a b c d e

2

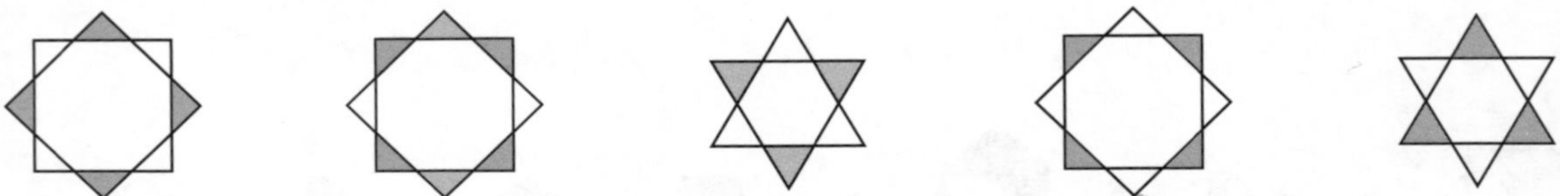

a b c d e

3

a b c d e

4

a b c d e

5

a b c d e

/ 5

Section 2 — Complete the Pair

The first figure in each question changes to become the second figure. Work out how the first figure has been changed. Then find the figure on the right that would match the third figure if it was changed in the same way.

Example:

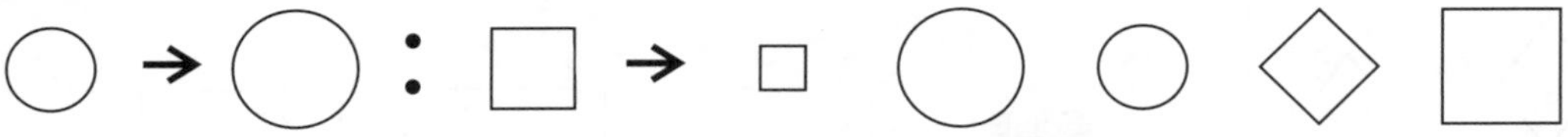

a b c d e

Answer: e

(1)

a b c d e

(2)

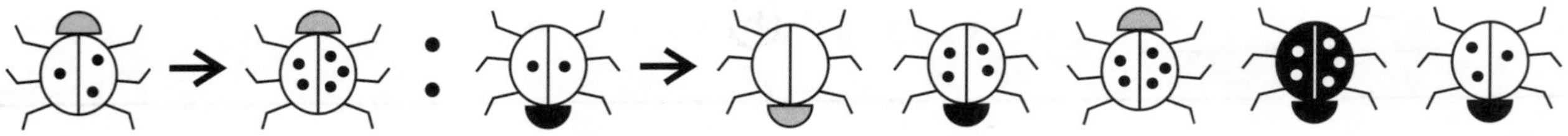

a b c d e

(3)

a b c d e

(4)

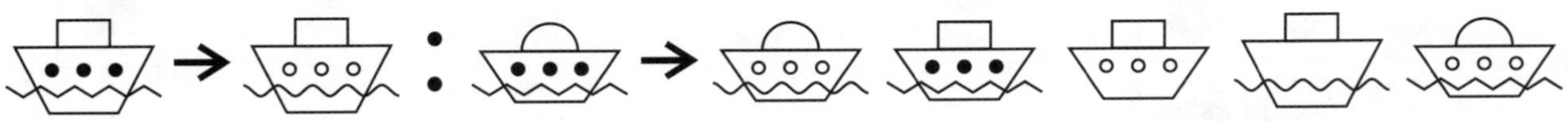

a b c d e

(5)

a b c d e

/ 5

Section 3 — Complete the Grid

On the left of each question below is a grid with one empty square.
Work out which of the five squares on the right should replace the empty square.

Example:

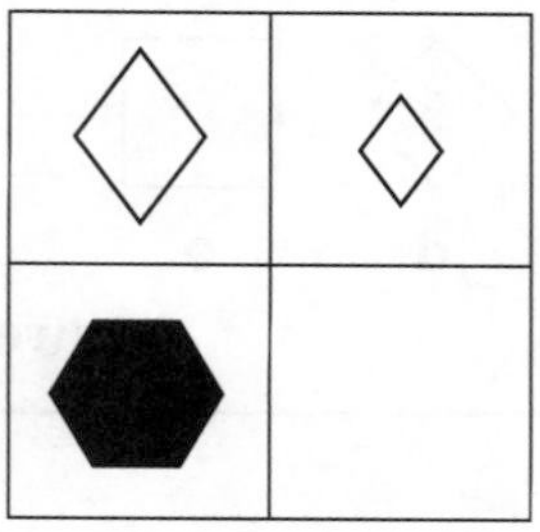

a b c d e

Answer: c

(1)

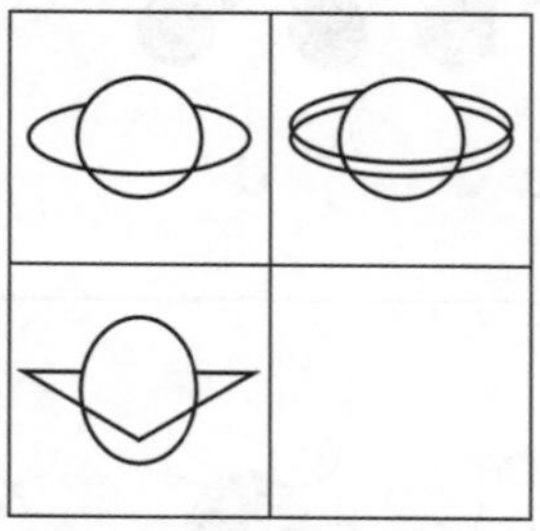

a b c d e

(2)

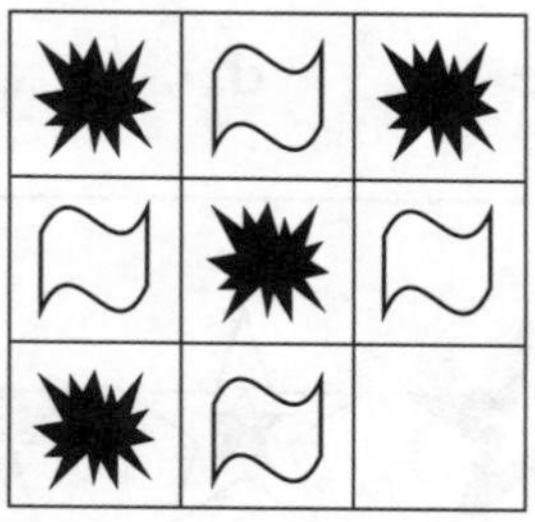

a b c d e

(3)

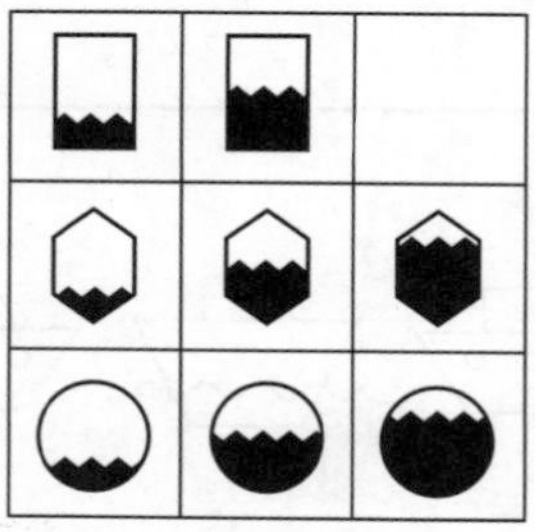

a b c d e

(4)

a b c d e

/ 4

Section 4 — Find the Figure Like the First Two

In each question, there are two figures on the left that are like each other in some way. Work out which of the five figures on the right is most like the two figures on the left.

Example:

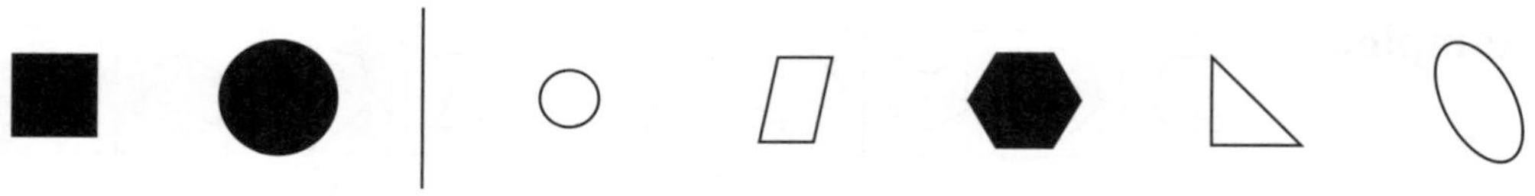

a b c d e

Answer: c

(1)

a b c d e

(2)

a b c d e

(3)

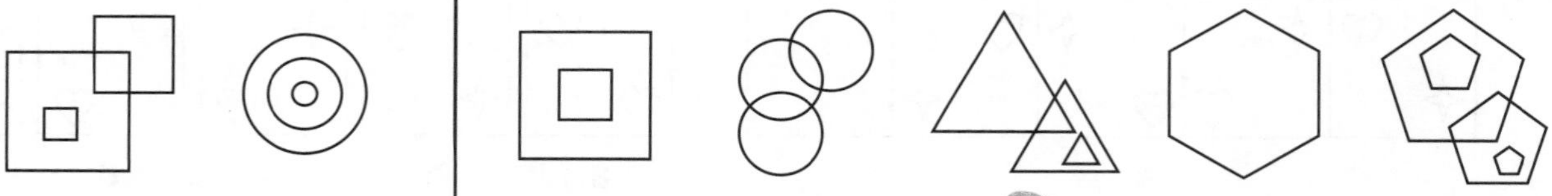

a b c d e

(4)

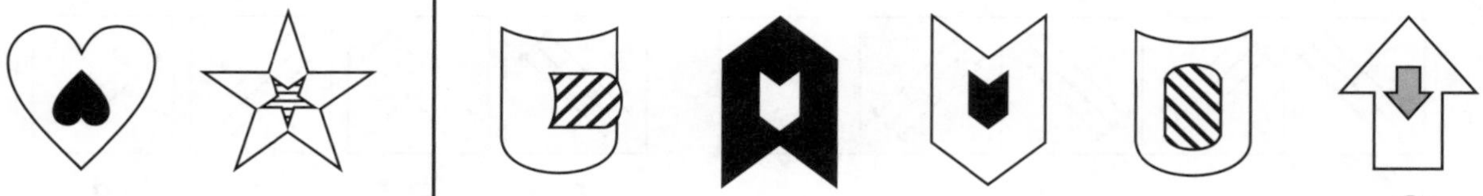

a b c d e

Not white on outside

(5)

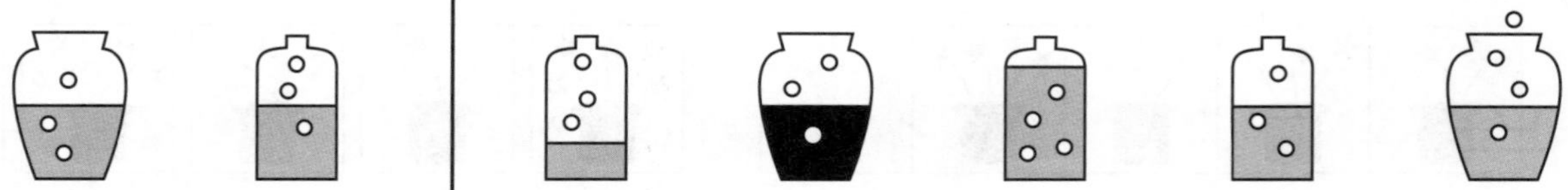

a b c d e

/ 5

Section 5 — Complete the Series

Each of these questions has five squares on the left that are arranged in order. One of the squares is empty. Work out which of the five squares on the right should replace the empty square.

Example:

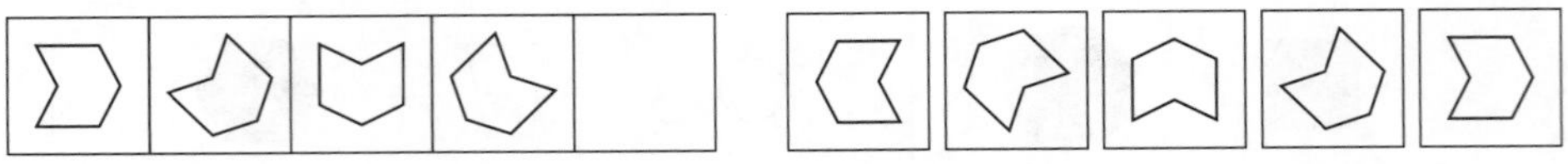

a b c d e

Answer: a

1

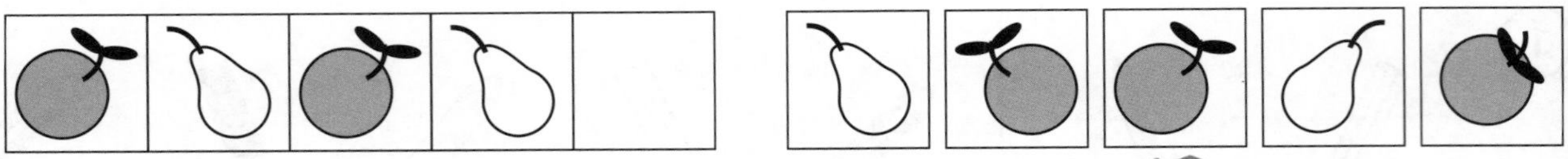

a b c d e

2

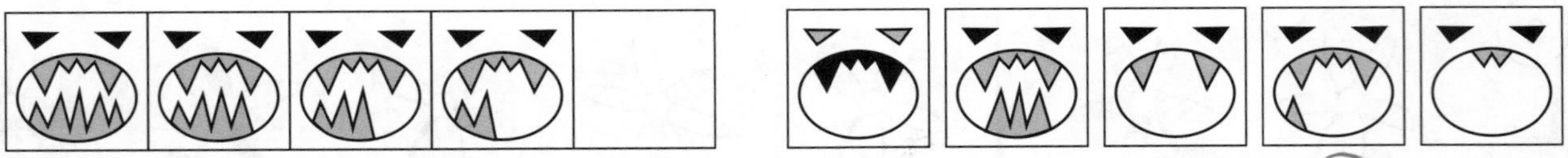

a b c d e

3

a b c d e

4

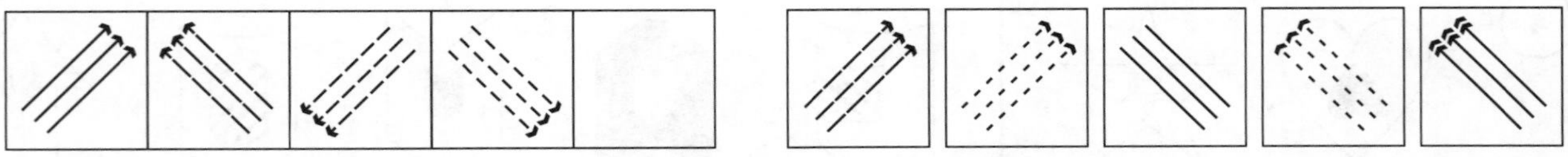

a b c d e

5

a b c d e

/ 5

Section 6 — Vertical Code

Each question has three figures on the left with code letters that describe them. You need to work out what the code letters mean. The figure on the right is missing its code. Work out which of the five codes on the right describes this figure.

Example:

P

Q

R

P	Q	T	S	R
a	**b**	**c**	**d**	**e**

Answer: a

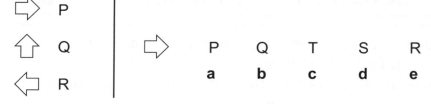

The arrow pointing right has the code letter P. The arrow pointing up has the code letter Q. The arrow pointing left has the code letter R. The figure on the right is an arrow pointing right, so its code must be P and the answer is **a**.

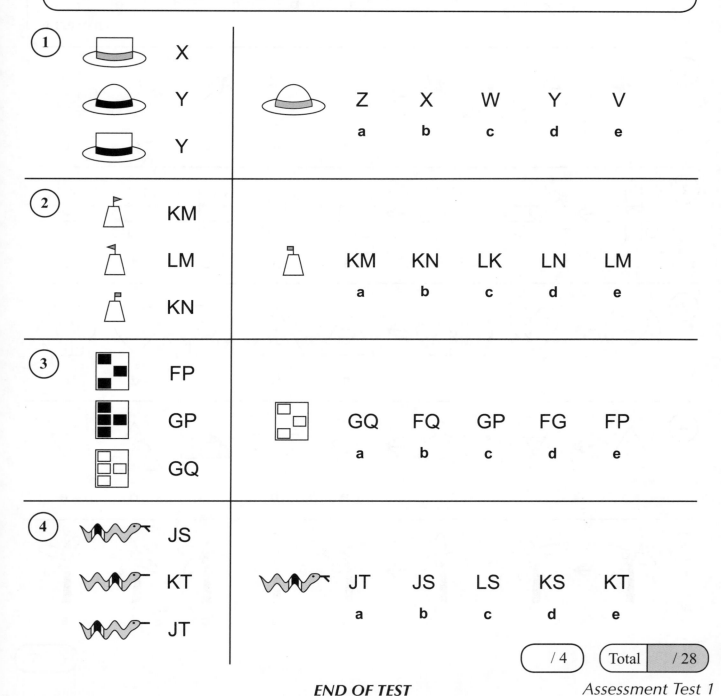

1.

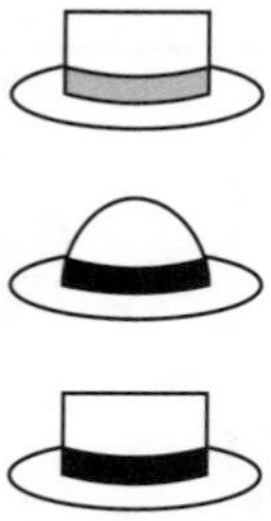

X

Y

Y

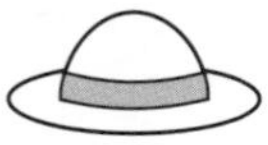

Z	X	W	Y	V
a	**b**	**c**	**d**	**e**

2.

KM

LM

KN

KM	KN	LK	LN	LM
a	**b**	**c**	**d**	**e**

3.

FP

GP

GQ

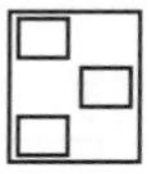

GQ	FQ	GP	FG	FP
a	**b**	**c**	**d**	**e**

4.

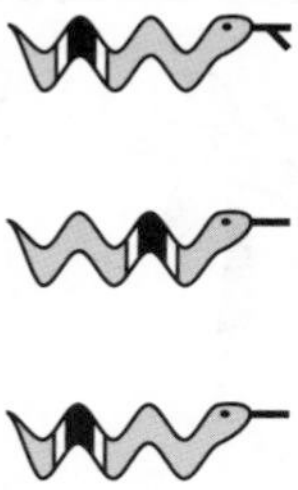

JS

KT

JT

JT	JS	LS	KS	KT
a	**b**	**c**	**d**	**e**

/ 4 Total / 28

END OF TEST

Assessment Test 2

You can print **multiple-choice answer sheets** for these questions from our website — go to www.cgplearning.co.uk/11+. If you'd prefer to answer them in standard write-in format, just circle the letter underneath your answer. The test should take around 15 minutes.

Section 1 — Complete the Pair

The first figure in each question changes to become the second figure. Work out how the first figure has been changed. Then find the figure on the right that would match the third figure if it was changed in the same way.

Example:

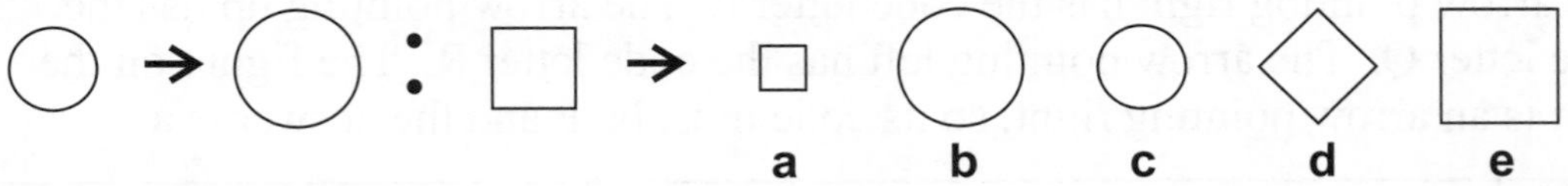

Answer: e

(1)

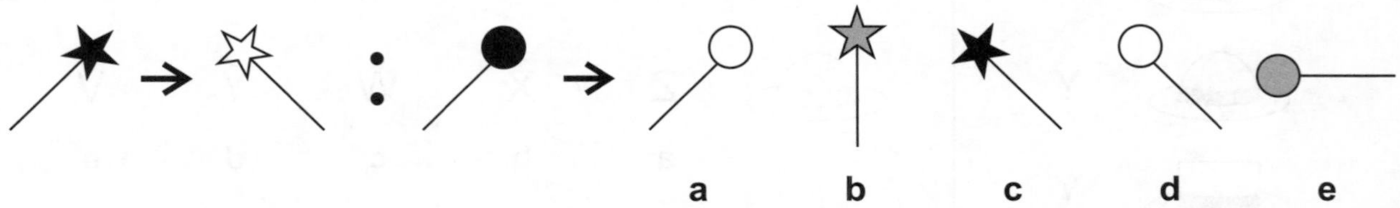

(2)

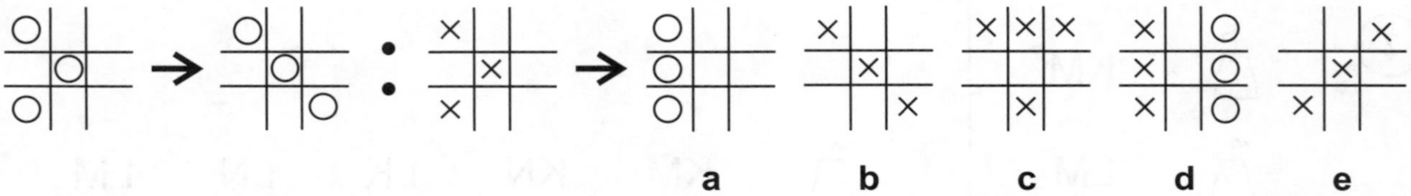

(3)

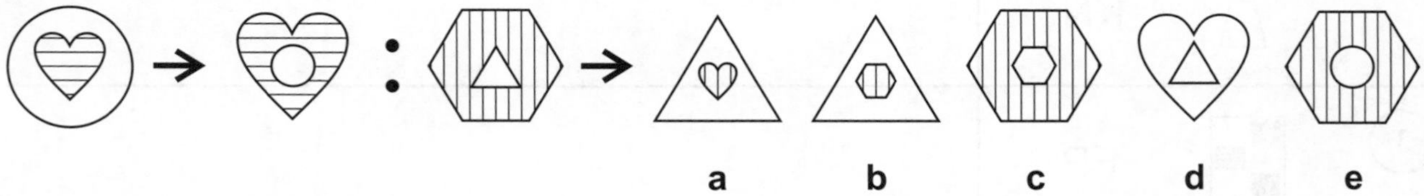

(4)

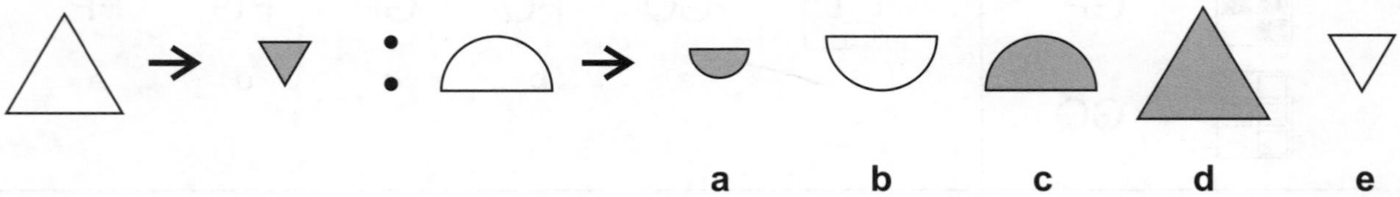

(5)

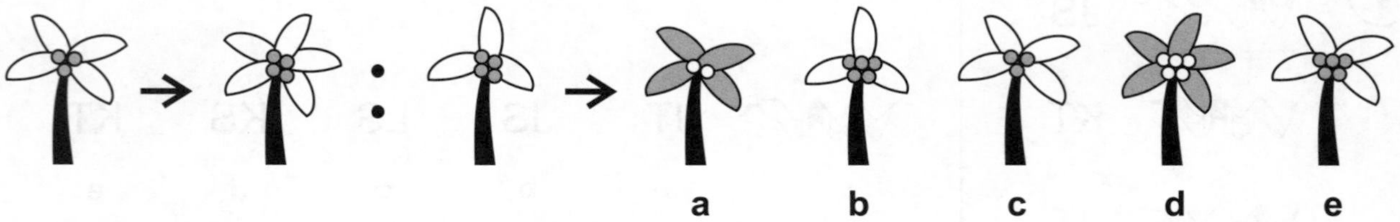

/ 5

Section 2 — Complete the Series

Each of these questions has five squares on the left that are arranged in order. One of the squares is empty. Work out which of the five squares on the right should replace the empty square.

Example:

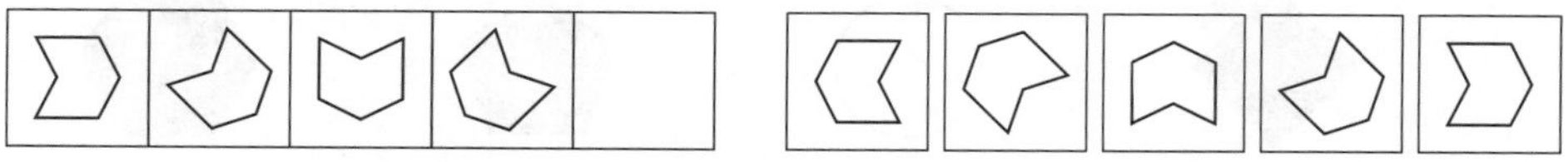

a b c d e

Answer: a

1

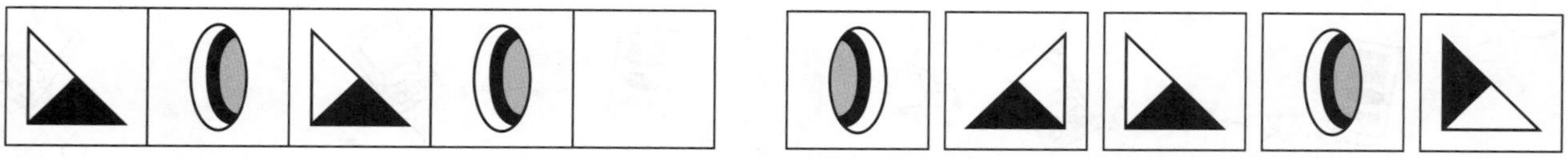

a b c d e

2

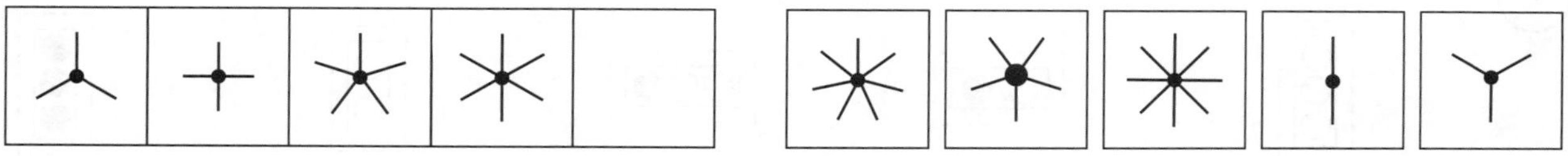

a b c d e

3

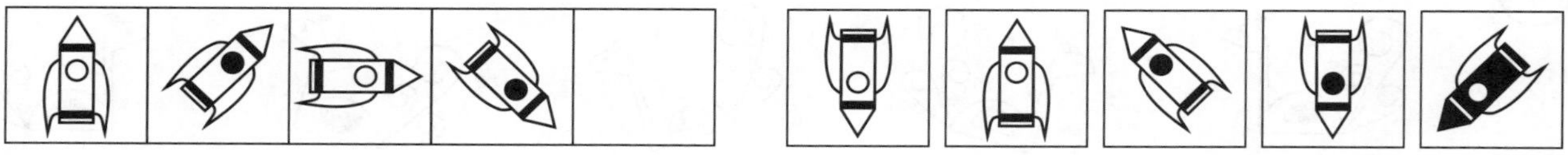

a b c d e

4

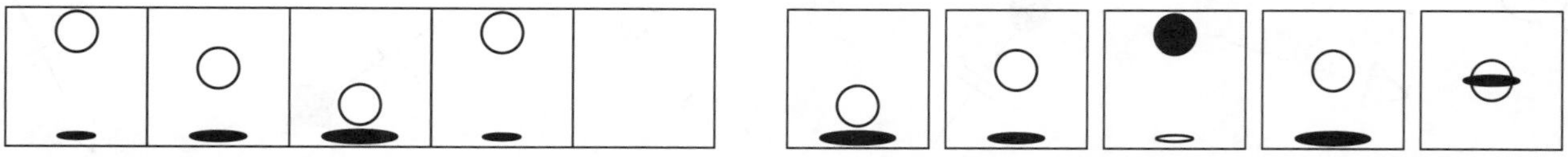

a b c d e

5

a b c d e

/ 5

Section 3 — Odd One Out

Each of the questions below has five figures.
Find the figure in each row that is most unlike the others.

Example:

a b c d e

Answer: b

(1)

a b c d e

(2)

a b c d e

(3)

a b c d e

(4)

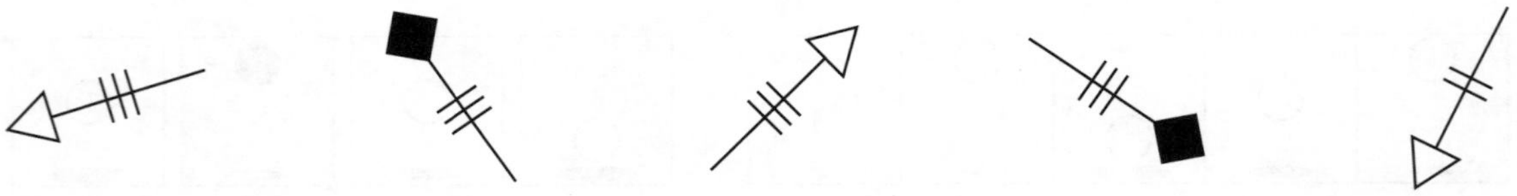

a b c d e

(5)

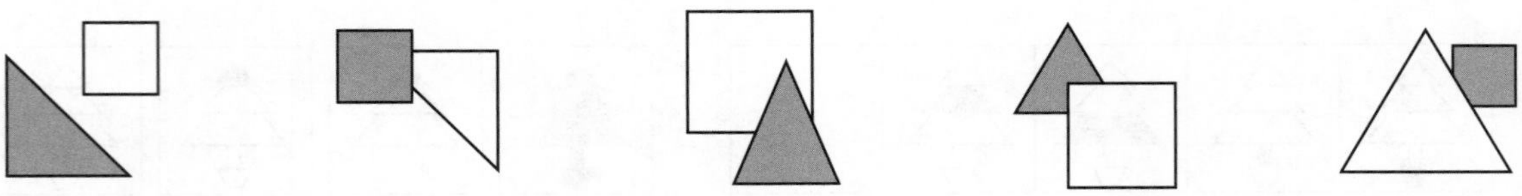

a b c d e

/ 5

Section 4 — Vertical Code

Each question has three figures on the left with code letters that describe them. You need to work out what the code letters mean. The figure on the right is missing its code. Work out which of the five codes on the right describes this figure.

Example:

P

Q

R

P	Q	T	S	R
a	**b**	**c**	**d**	**e**

Answer: a

The arrow pointing right has the code letter P. The arrow pointing up has the code letter Q. The arrow pointing left has the code letter R. The figure on the right is an arrow pointing right, so its code must be P and the answer is **a**.

1.

M

L

M

P	L	N	M	R
a	**b**	**c**	**d**	**e**

2.

XZ

YZ

XW

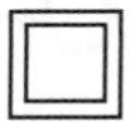

YZ	YW	YX	XY	XW
a	**b**	**c**	**d**	**e**

3.

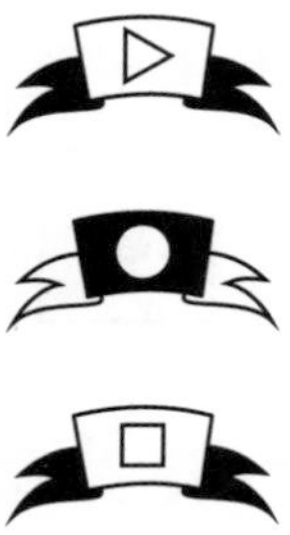

AP

CQ

BP

BQ	CP	BP	AB	AQ
a	**b**	**c**	**d**	**e**

4.

ES

GT

FS

EG	EF	GS	FT	ET
a	**b**	**c**	**d**	**e**

/ 4

Section 5 — Complete the Grid

On the left of each question below is a grid with one empty square.
Work out which of the five squares on the right should replace the empty square.

Example:

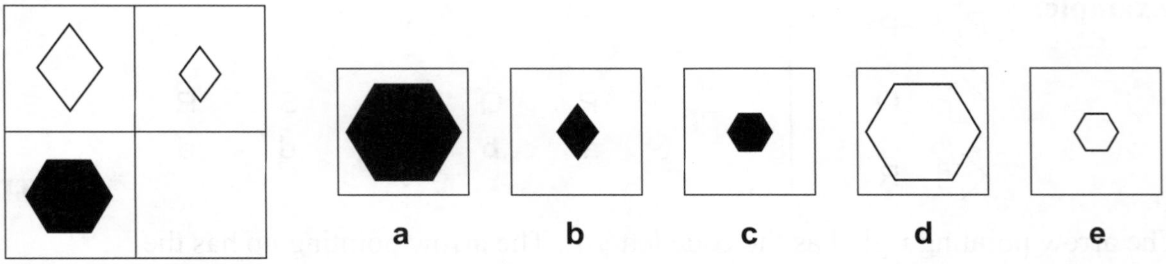

Answer: c

(1)

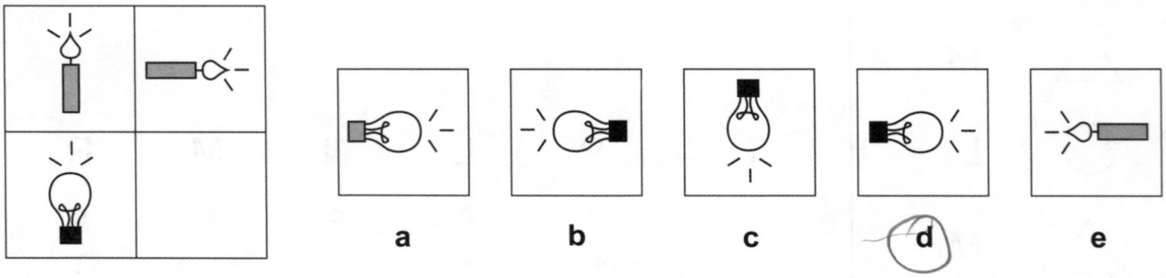

(2)

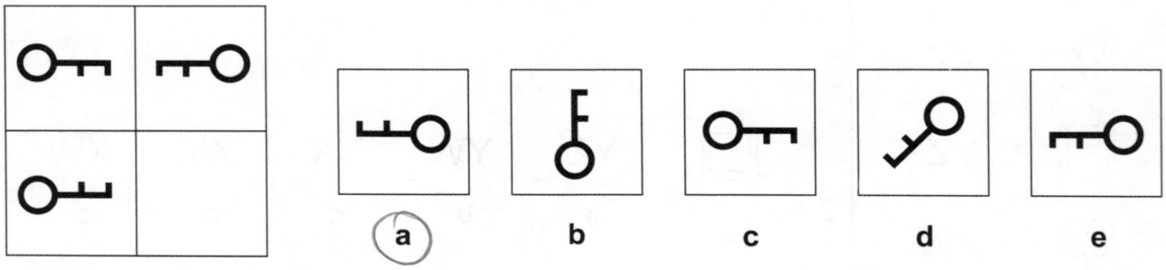

(3)

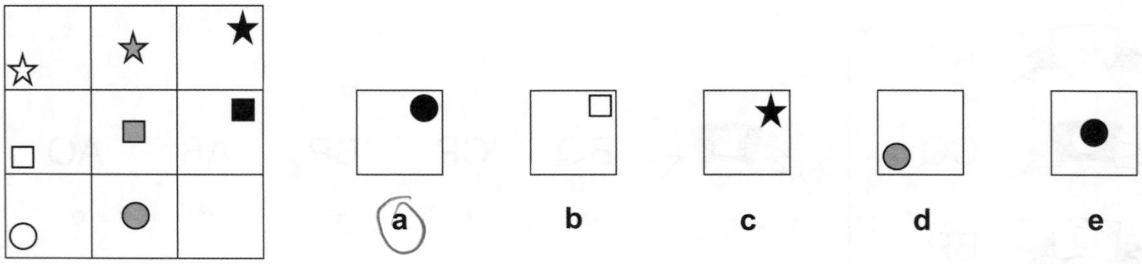

(4)

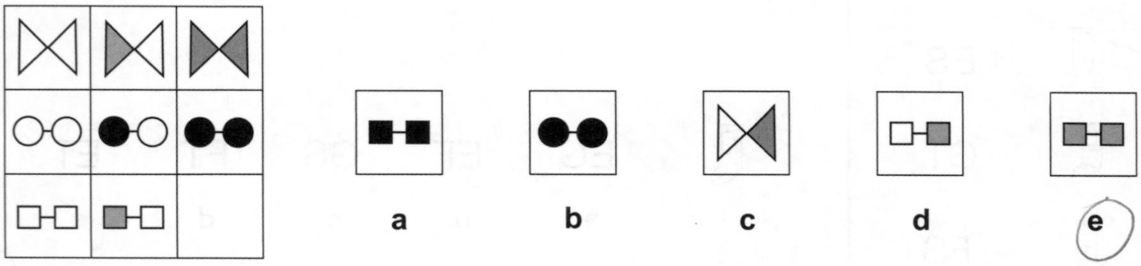

/ 4

Section 6 — Find the Figure Like the First Three

In each question, there are three figures on the left that are like each other in some way. Work out which of the five figures on the right is most like the three figures on the left.

Example:

a b c d e

Answer: c

(1)

a b c d e

(2)

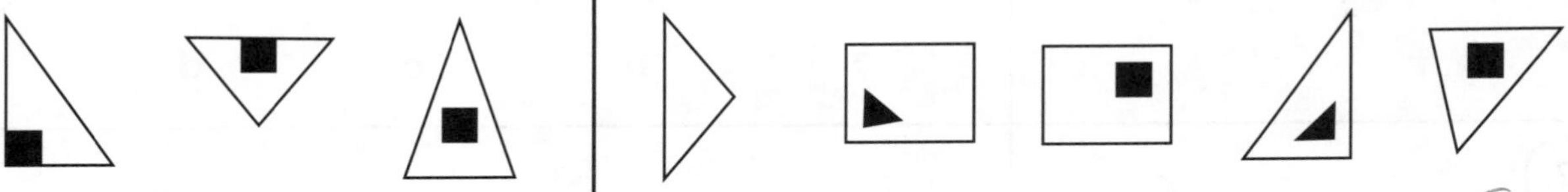

a b c d e

(3)

a b c d e

(4)

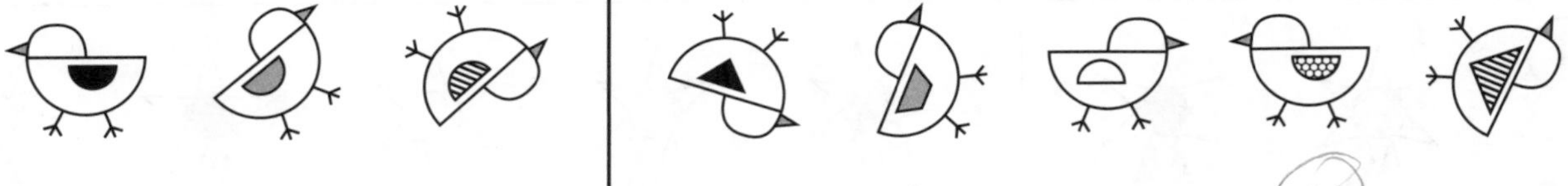

a b c d e

(5)

a b c d e

5 / 5 Total / 28

Assessment Test 3

You can print **multiple-choice answer sheets** for these questions from our website — go to www.cgplearning.co.uk/11+. If you'd prefer to answer them in standard write-in format, just circle the letter underneath your answer. The test should take around 15 minutes.

Section 1 — Find the Figure Like the First Two

In each question, there are two figures on the left that are like each other in some way. Work out which of the five figures on the right is most like the two figures on the left.

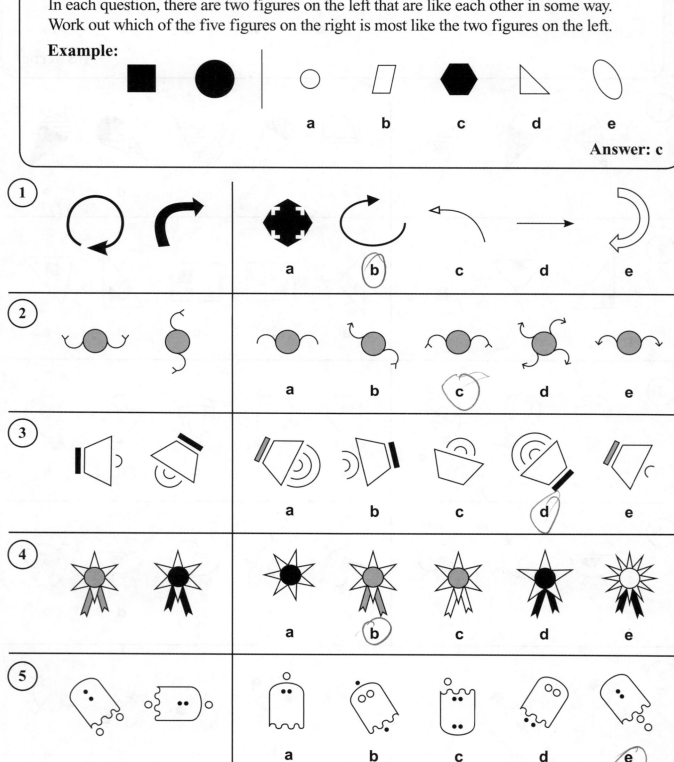

Example:

a b c d e

Answer: c

(1)

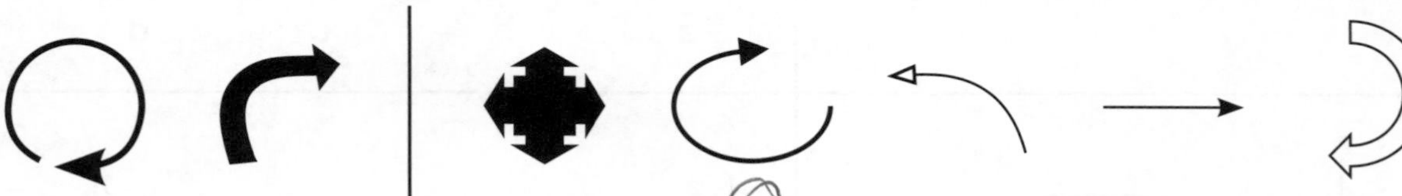

a b c d e

(2)

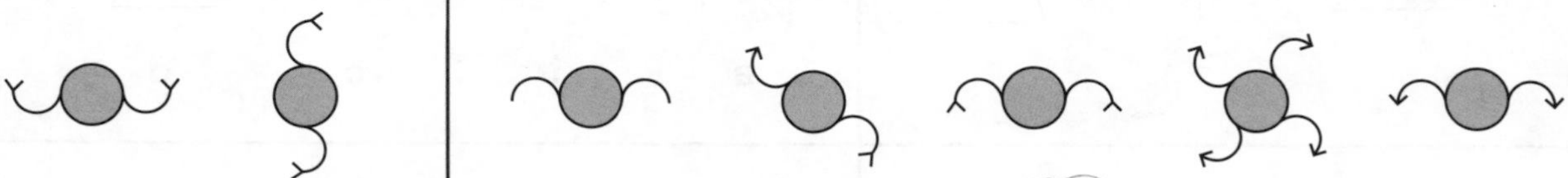

a b c d e

(3)

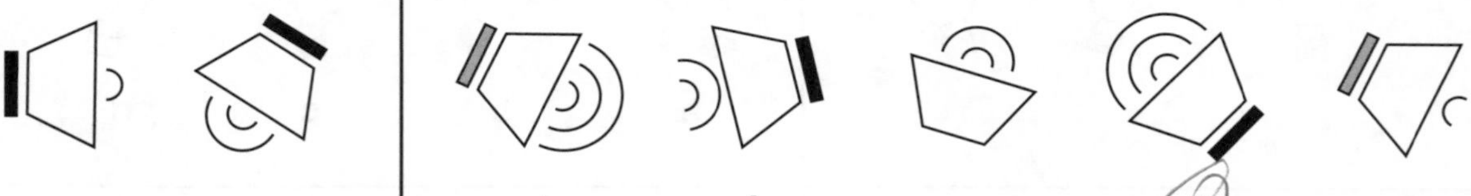

a b c d e

(4)

a b c d e

(5)

a b c d e

5 / 5

Section 2 — Vertical Code

Each question has three figures on the left with code letters that describe them. You need to work out what the code letters mean. The figure on the right is missing its code. Work out which of the five codes on the right describes this figure.

Example:

P

Q

R

P	Q	T	S	R
a	**b**	**c**	**d**	**e**

Answer: a

The arrow pointing right has the code letter P. The arrow pointing up has the code letter Q. The arrow pointing left has the code letter R. The figure on the right is an arrow pointing right, so its code must be P and the answer is **a**.

1

F

H

G

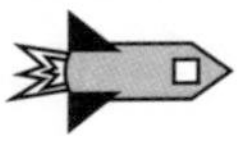

K	H	F	G	J
a	**b**	**c**	**d**	**e**

2

HZ

JY

HY

HY	JZ	HZ	JX	JY
a	**b**	**c**	**d**	**e**

3

AV

BW

CV

CW	AV	BV	CV	AW
a	**b**	**c**	**d**	**e**

4

CY

DX

BX

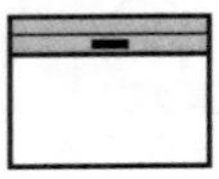

DY	BX	CX	BY	DX
a	**b**	**c**	**d**	**e**

4 / 4

Section 3 — Complete the Series

Each of these questions has five squares on the left that are arranged in order. One of the squares is empty. Work out which of the five squares on the right should replace the empty square.

Example:

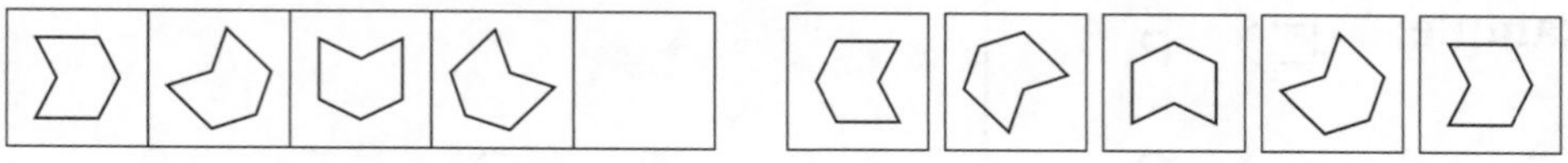

a b c d e

Answer: a

1

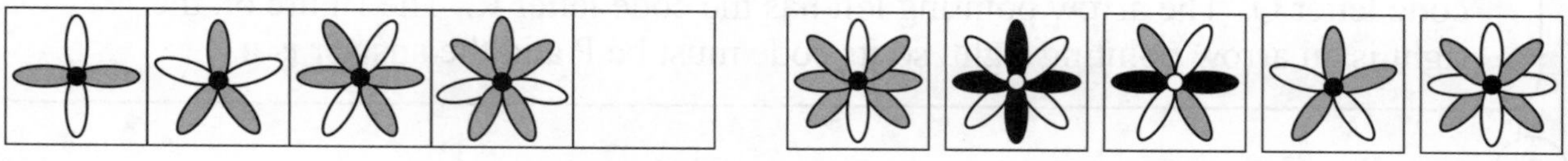

a b c d e

2

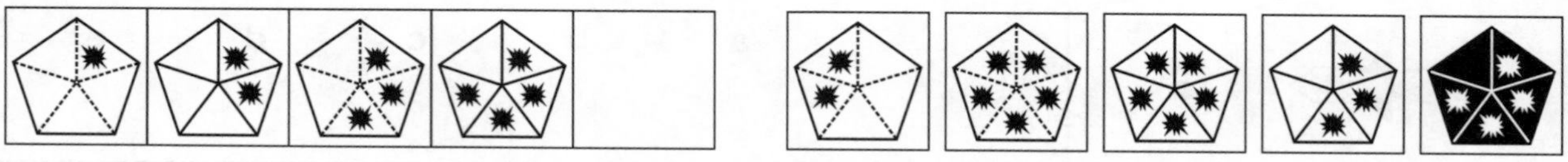

a b c d e

3

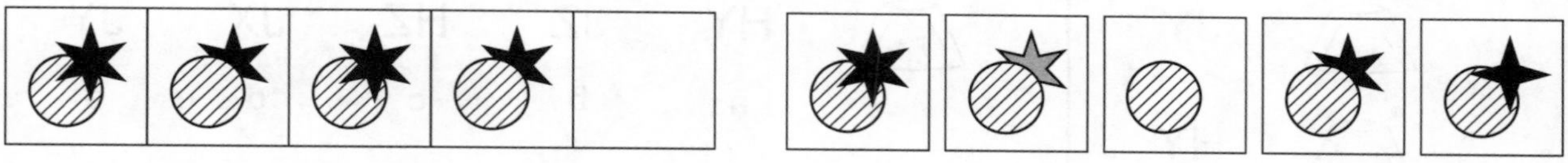

a b c d e

4

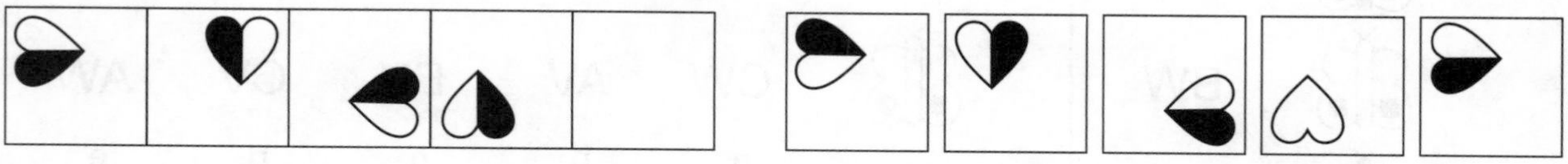

a b c d e

5

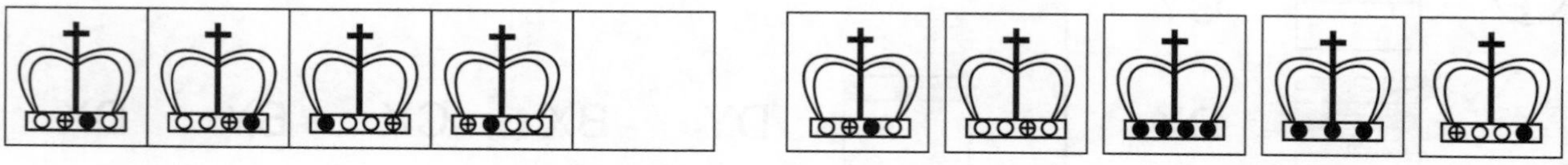

a b c d e

/ 5

Section 4 — Complete the Grid

On the left of each question below is a grid with one empty square.
Work out which of the five squares on the right should replace the empty square.

Example:

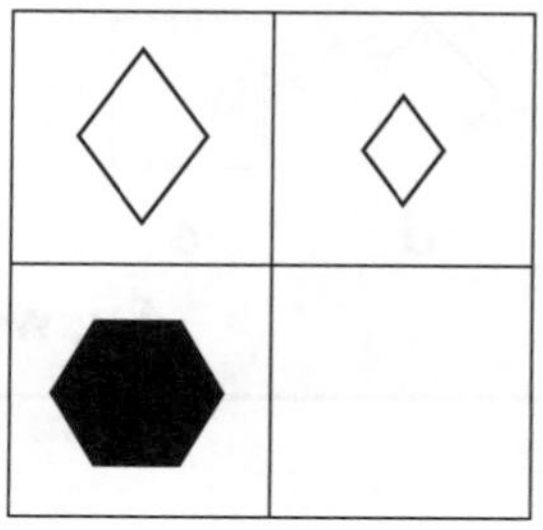

a b c d e

Answer: c

1

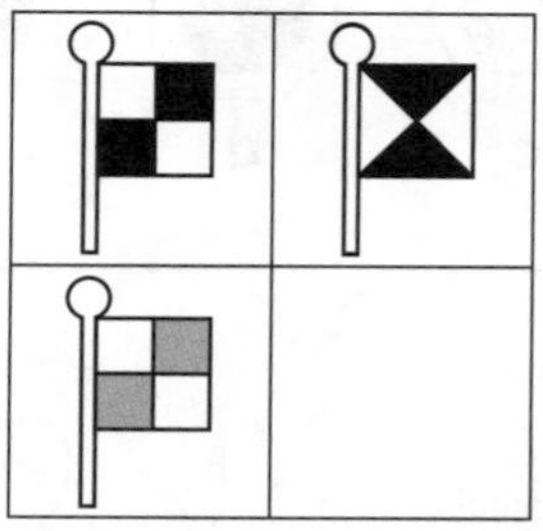

a b c d e

2

a b c d e

3

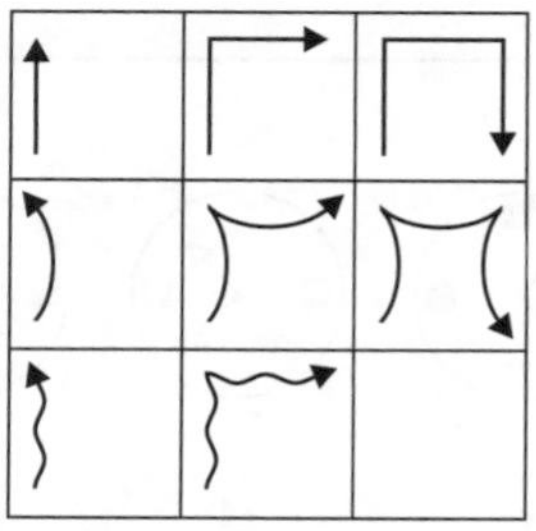

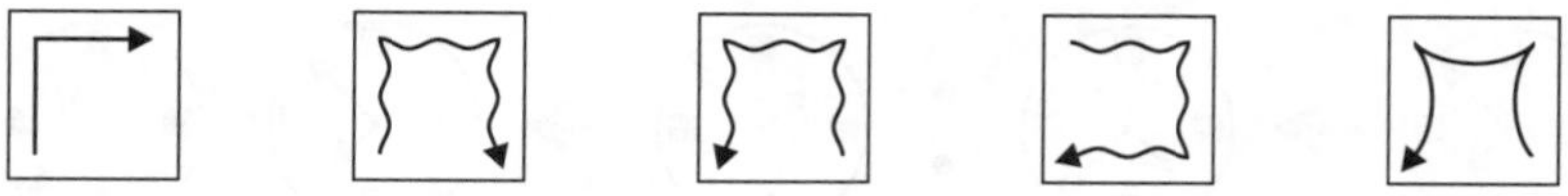

a b c d e

4

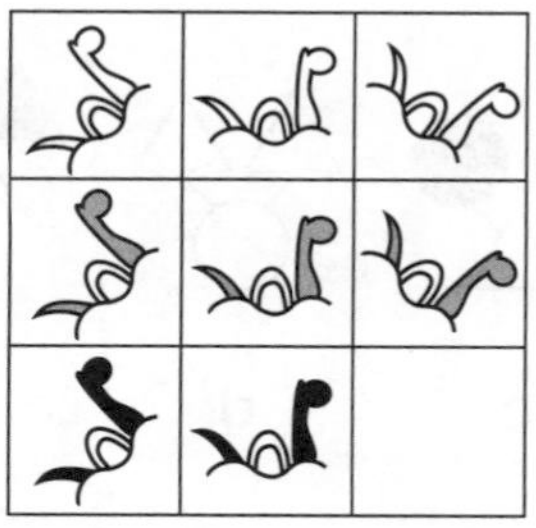

a b c d e

/ 4

Section 5 — Complete the Pair

The first figure in each question changes to become the second figure. Work out how the first figure has been changed. Then find the figure on the right that would match the third figure if it was changed in the same way.

Example:

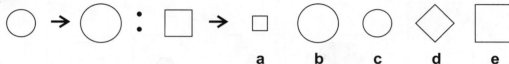

a b c d e

Answer: e

(1)

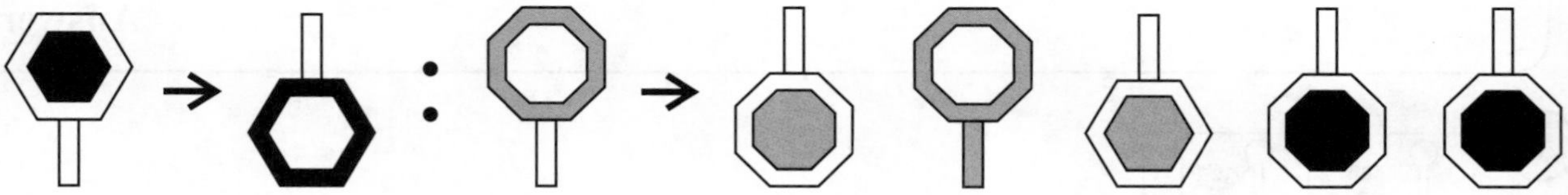

a b c d e

(2)

a b c d e

(3)

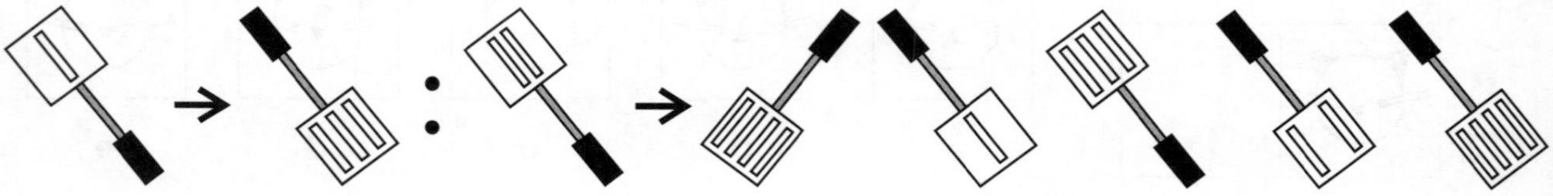

a b c d e

(4)

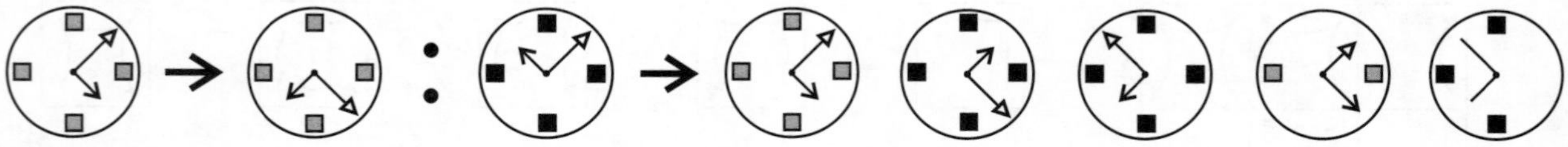

a b c d e

(5)

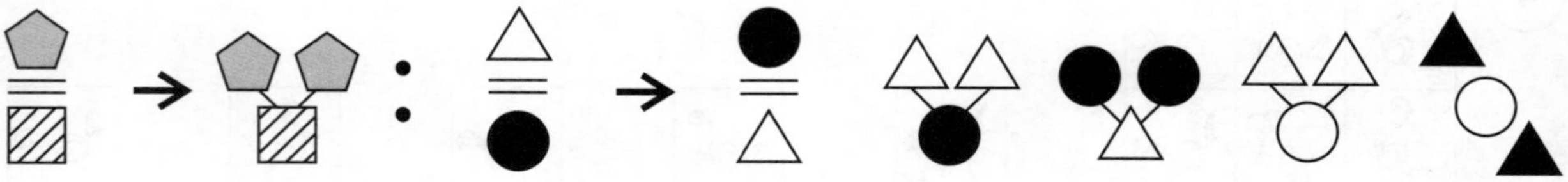

a b c d e

/ 5

Section 6 — Odd One Out

Each of the questions below has five figures.
Find the figure in each row that is most unlike the others.

Example:

a b c d e

Answer: b

(1)

a b c d e

(2)

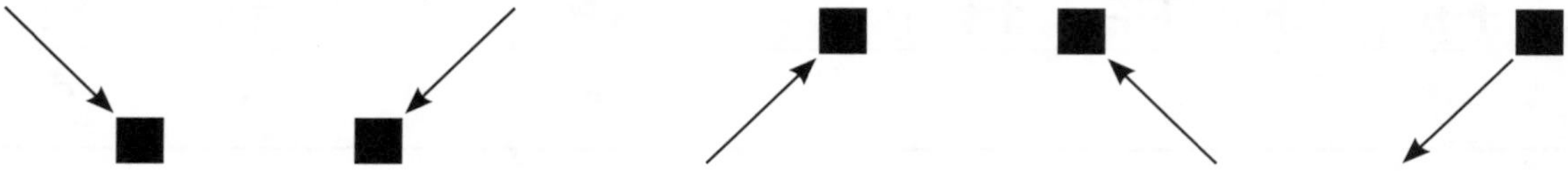

a b c d e

(3)

a b c d e

(4)

a b c d e

(5)

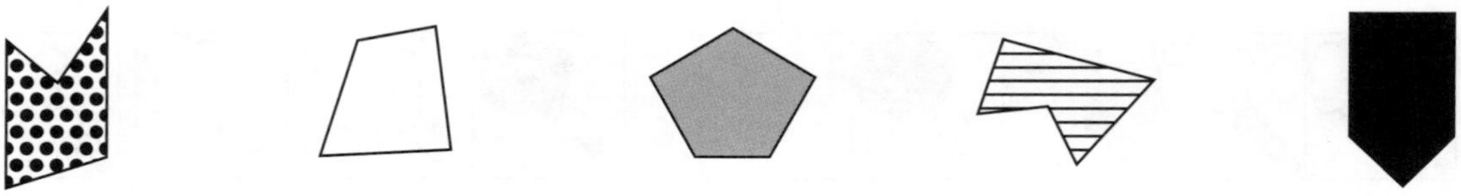

a b c d e

/ 5 Total / 28

END OF TEST

Assessment Test 4

You can print **multiple-choice answer sheets** for these questions from our website — go to www.cgplearning.co.uk/11+. If you'd prefer to answer them in standard write-in format, just circle the letter underneath your answer. The test should take around 15 minutes.

Section 1 — Complete the Series

Each of these questions has five squares on the left that are arranged in order. One of the squares is empty. Work out which of the five squares on the right should replace the empty square.

Example:

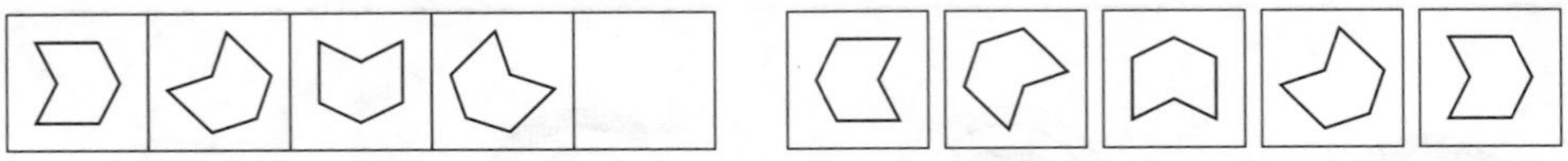

a b c d e

Answer: a

1

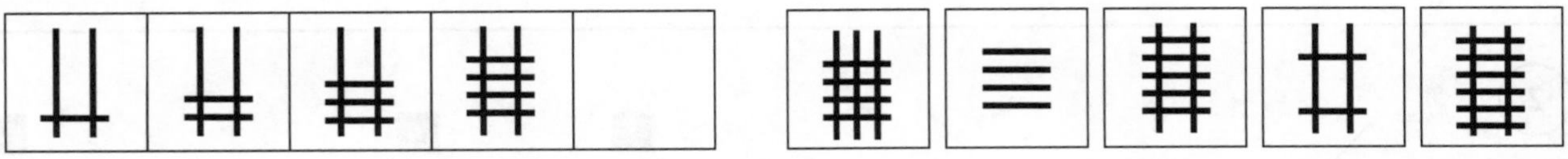

a b c d e

2

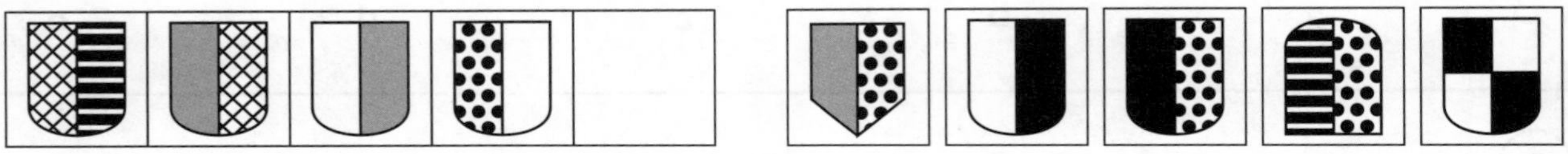

a b c d e

3

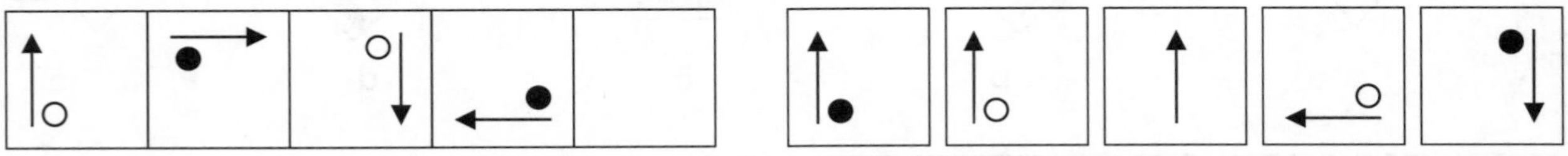

a b c d e

4

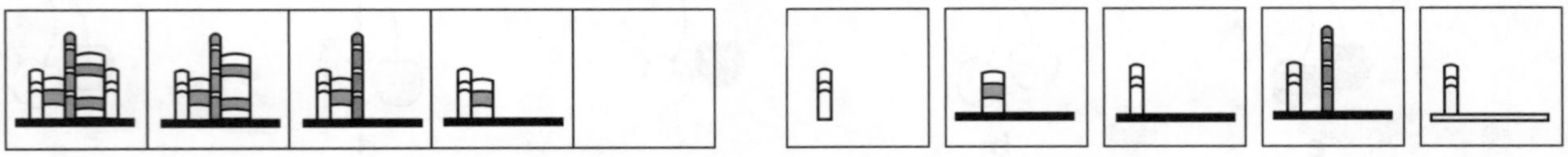

a b c d e

5

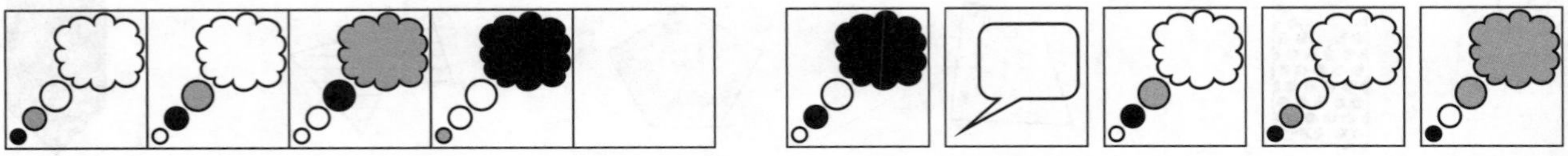

a b c d e

/ 5

Section 2 — Complete the Grid

On the left of each question below is a grid with one empty square.
Work out which of the five squares on the right should replace the empty square.

Example:

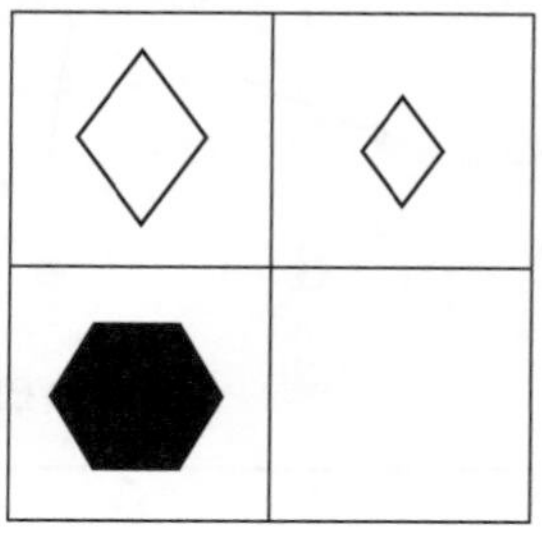

a b c d e

Answer: c

(1)

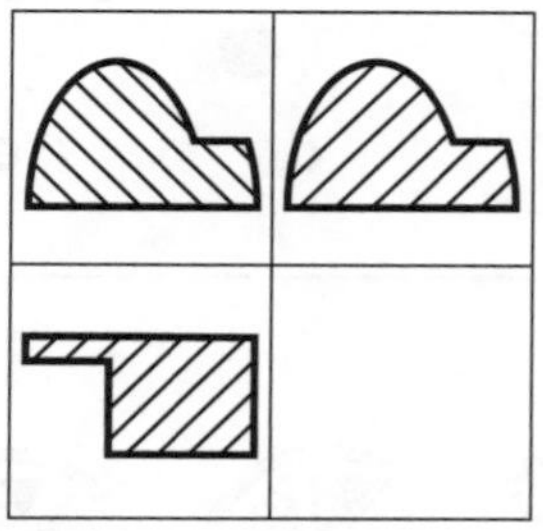

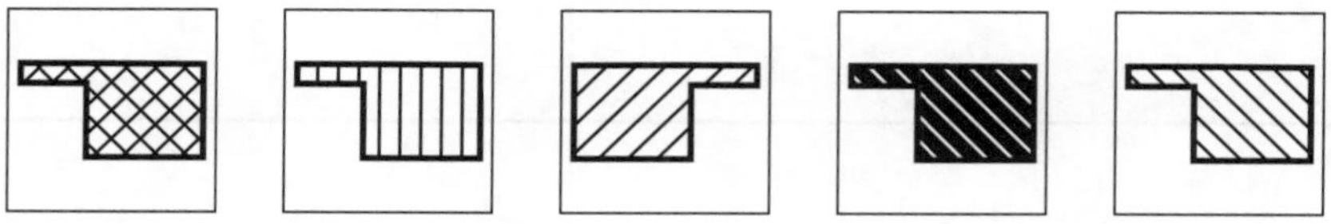

a b c d e

(2)

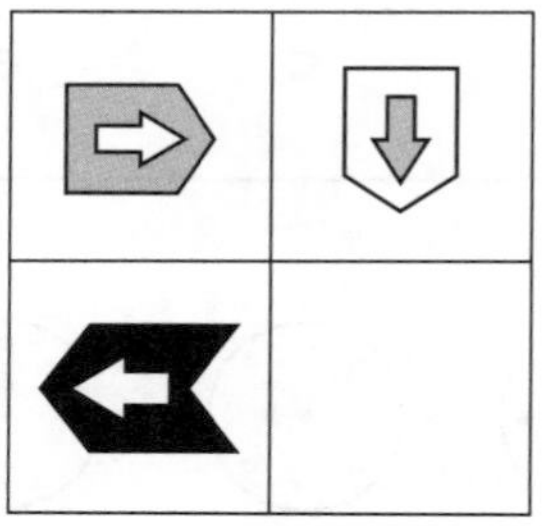

a b c d e

(3)

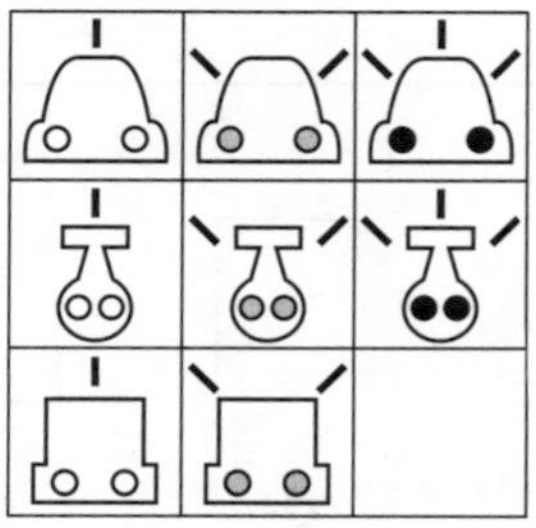

a b c d e

(4)

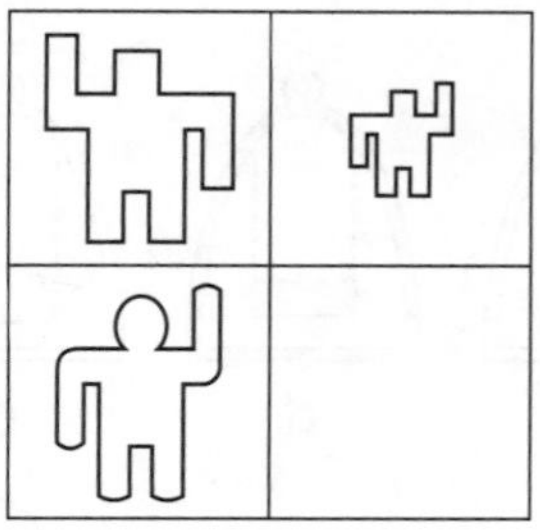

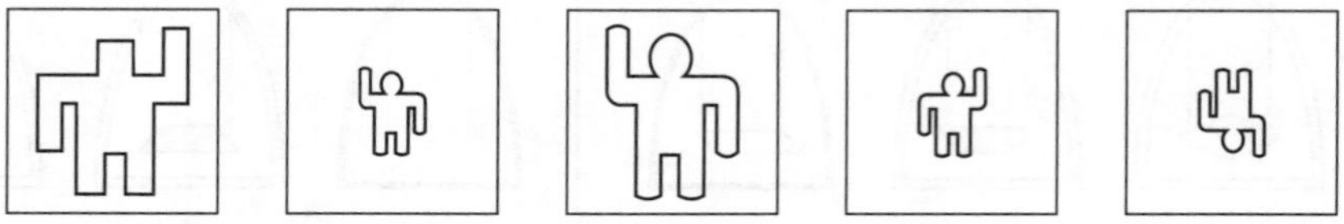

a b c d e

/ 4

Section 3 — Find the Figure Like the First Three

In each question, there are three figures on the left that are like each other in some way. Work out which of the five figures on the right is most like the three figures on the left.

Example:

a b c d e

Answer: c

(1)

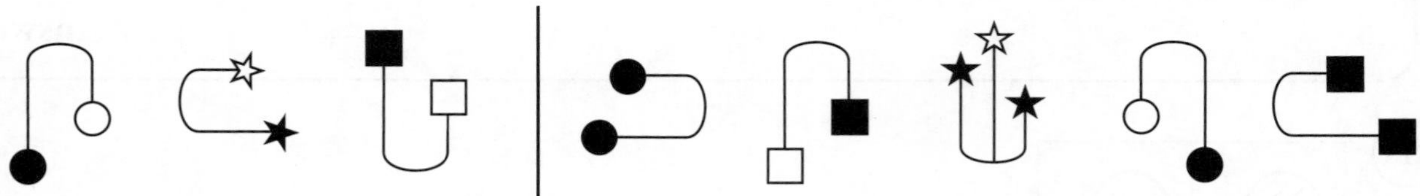

a b c d e

(2)

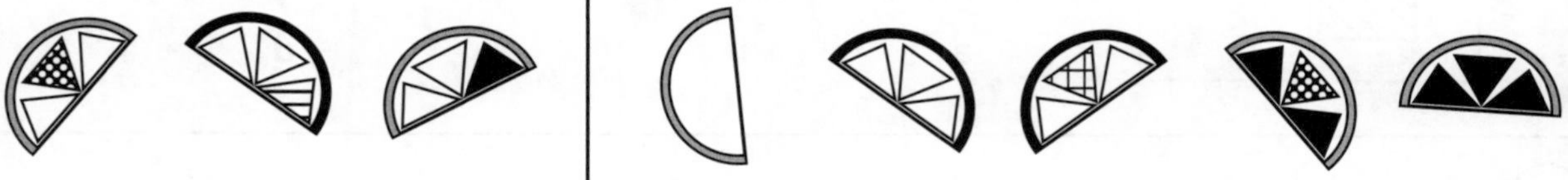

a b c d e

(3)

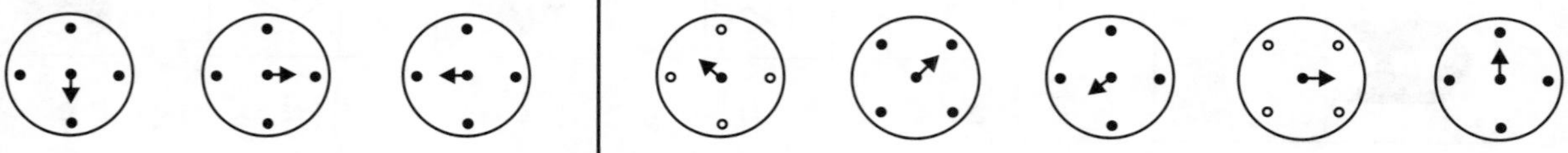

a b c d e

(4)

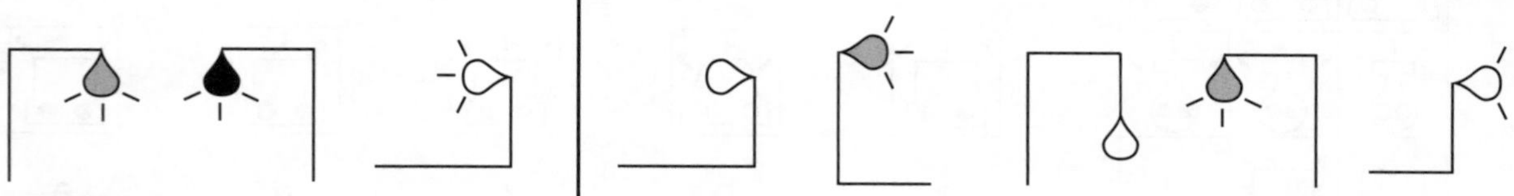

a b c d e

(5)

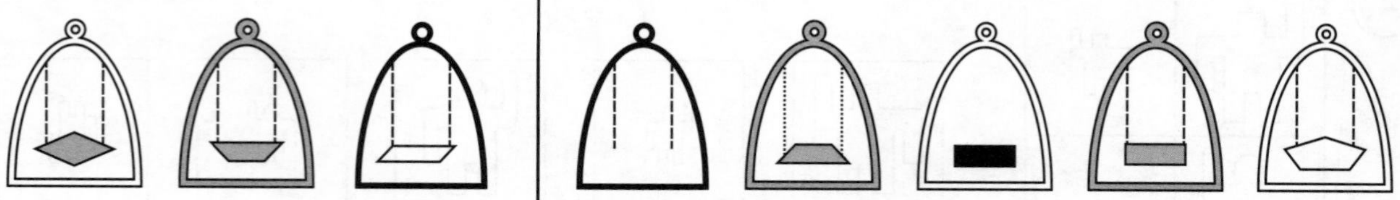

a b c d e

/ 5

Section 4 — Odd One Out

Each of the questions below has five figures.
Find the figure in each row that is most unlike the others.

Example:

a b c d e

Answer: b

1

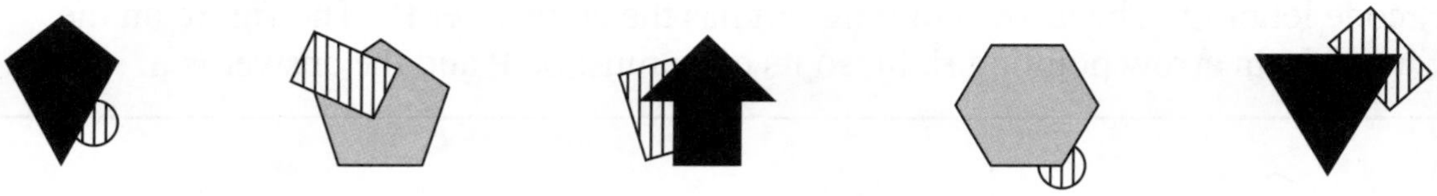

a b c d e

2

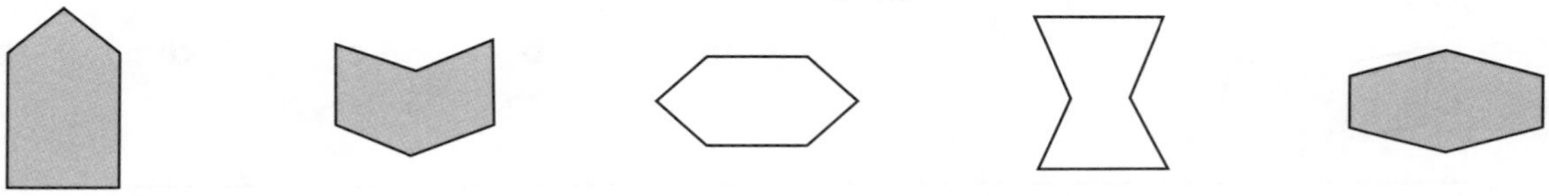

a b c d e

3

a b c d e

4

a b c d e

5

a b c d e

/ 5

Section 5 — Vertical Code

Each question has three figures on the left with code letters that describe them. You need to work out what the code letters mean. The figure on the right is missing its code. Work out which of the five codes on the right describes this figure.

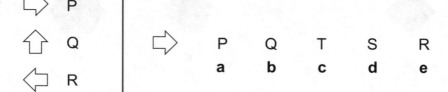

Example:

 P

 Q

 R

P	Q	T	S	R
a	**b**	**c**	**d**	**e**

Answer: a

The arrow pointing right has the code letter P. The arrow pointing up has the code letter Q. The arrow pointing left has the code letter R. The figure on the right is an arrow pointing right, so its code must be P and the answer is **a**.

1

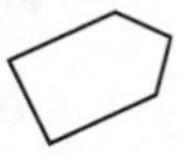 Z

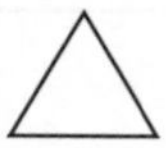 X

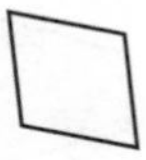 W

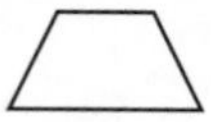

W	V	Z	Y	X
a	**b**	**c**	**d**	**e**

2

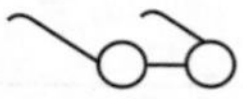 AY

 BX

 AX

AX	AY	BY	BX	AZ
a	**b**	**c**	**d**	**e**

3

 AW

 BW

 CV

CW	AW	BW	AV	BV
a	**b**	**c**	**d**	**e**

4

 AF

 CF

 BG

AG	CG	BF	AF	CF
a	**b**	**c**	**d**	**e**

/ 4

Section 6 — Complete the Pair

The first figure in each question changes to become the second figure. Work out how the first figure has been changed. Then find the figure on the right that would match the third figure if it was changed in the same way.

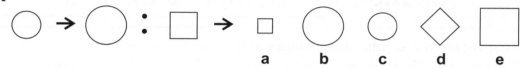

Example:

a b c d e

Answer: e

1

a b c d e

2

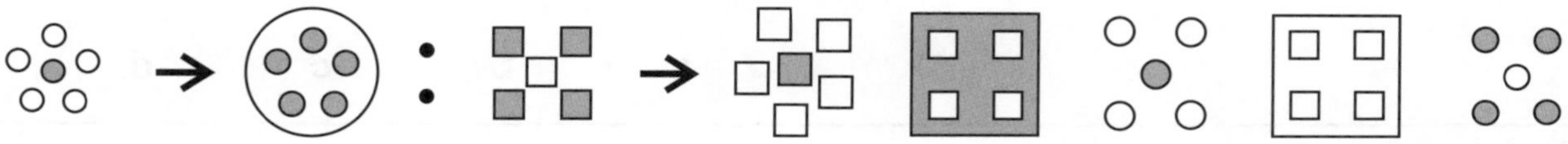

a b c d e

3

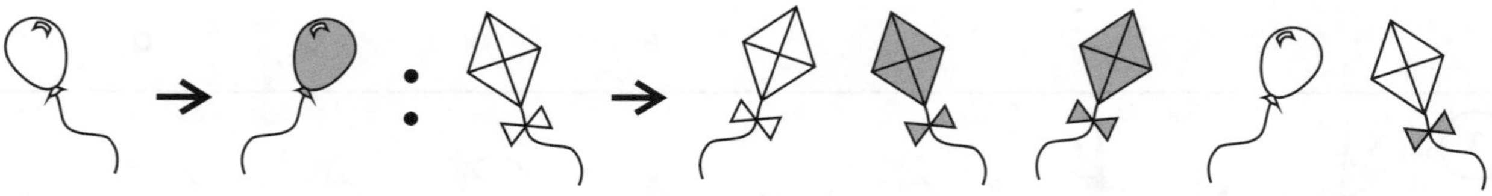

a b c d e

4

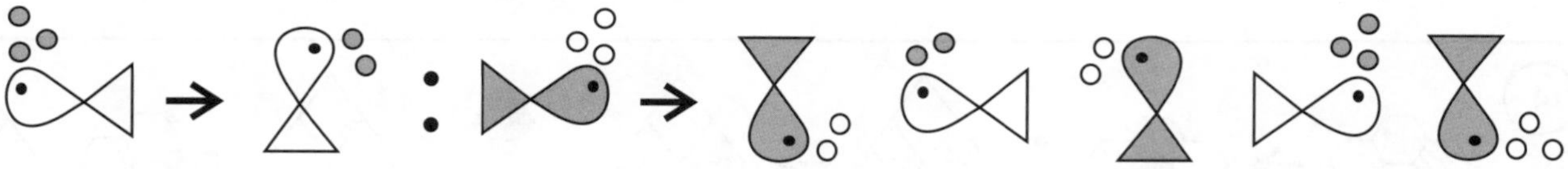

a b c d e

5

a b c d e

/ 5 Total / 28

Assessment Test 5

You can print **multiple-choice answer sheets** for these questions from our website — go to www.cgplearning.co.uk/11+. If you'd prefer to answer them in standard write-in format, just circle the letter underneath your answer. The test should take around 15 minutes.

Section 1 — Complete the Pair

The first figure in each question changes to become the second figure. Work out how the first figure has been changed. Then find the figure on the right that would match the third figure if it was changed in the same way.

Example:

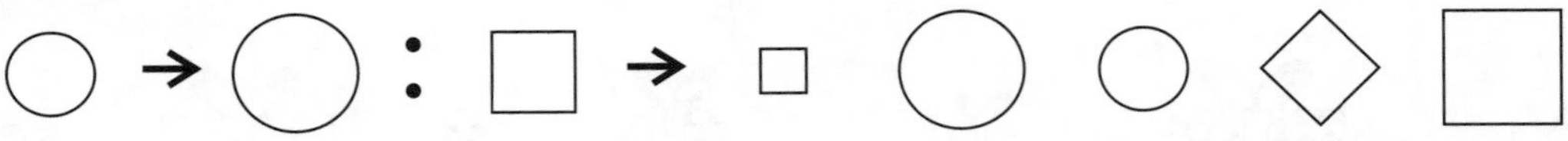

a b c d e

Answer: e

1

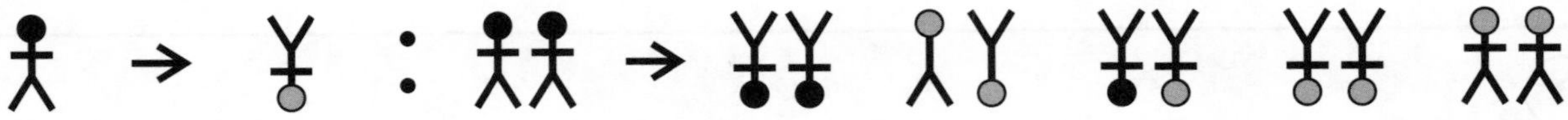

a b c d e

2

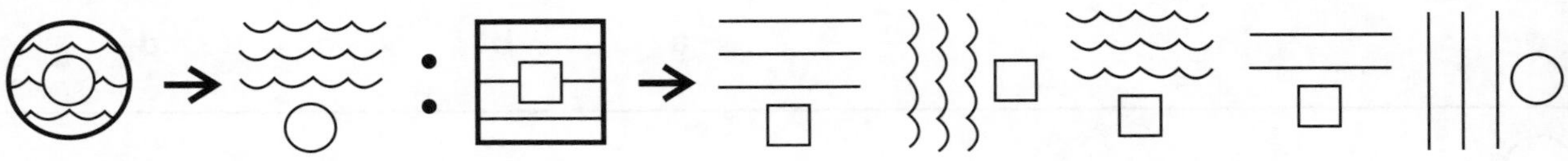

a b c d e

3

a b c d e

4

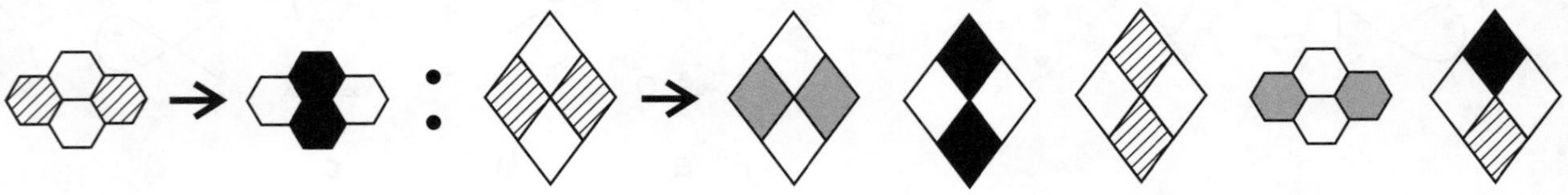

a b c d e

5

a b c d e

/ 5

Section 2 — Odd One Out

Each of the questions below has five figures.
Find the figure in each row that is most unlike the others.

Example:

a b c d e

Answer: b

(1)

a b c d e

(2)

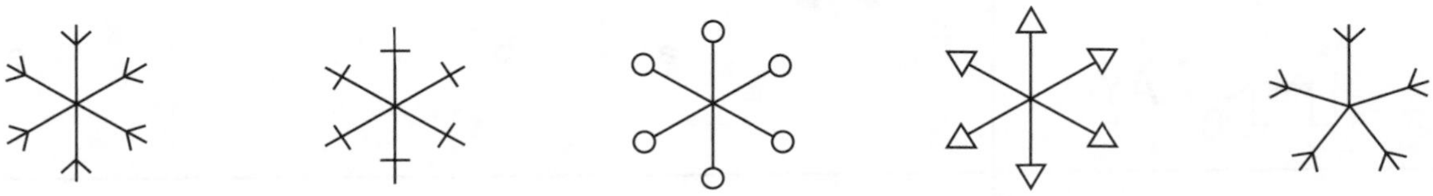

a b c d e

(3)

a b c d e

(4)

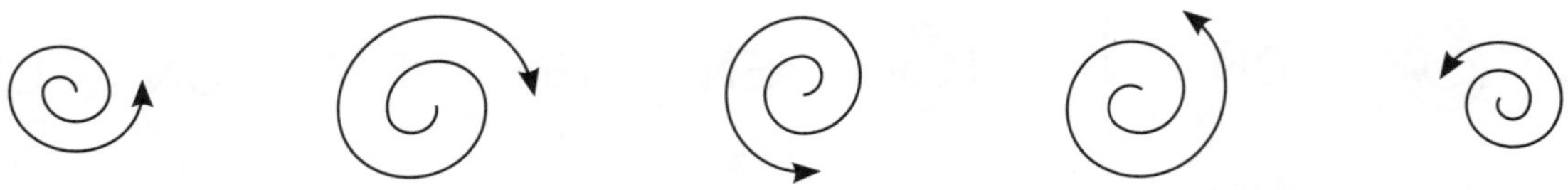

a b c d e

(5)

a b c d e

/ 5

Section 3 — Vertical Code

Each question has three figures on the left with code letters that describe them. You need to work out what the code letters mean. The figure on the right is missing its code. Work out which of the five codes on the right describes this figure.

Example:

P
Q
R

a	b	c	d	e
P	Q	T	S	R

Answer: a

The arrow pointing right has the code letter P. The arrow pointing up has the code letter Q. The arrow pointing left has the code letter R. The figure on the right is an arrow pointing right, so its code must be P and the answer is **a**.

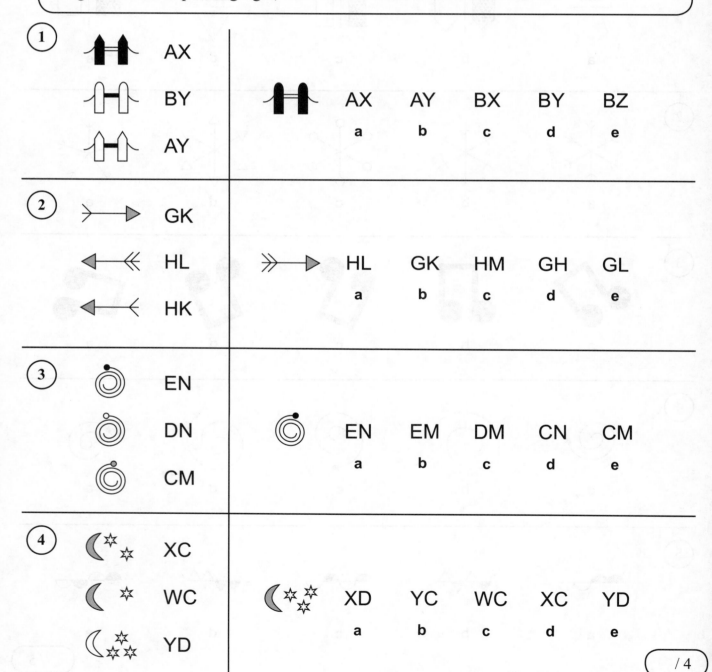

1

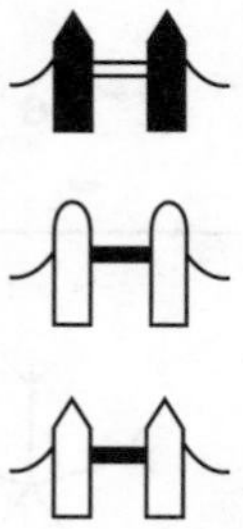

AX
BY
AY

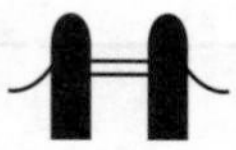

a	b	c	d	e
AX	AY	BX	BY	BZ

2

GK
HL
HK

a	b	c	d	e
HL	GK	HM	GH	GL

3

EN
DN
CM

a	b	c	d	e
EN	EM	DM	CN	CM

4

XC
WC
YD

a	b	c	d	e
XD	YC	WC	XC	YD

/ 4

Section 4 — Complete the Grid

On the left of each question below is a grid with one empty square.
Work out which of the five squares on the right should replace the empty square.

Example:

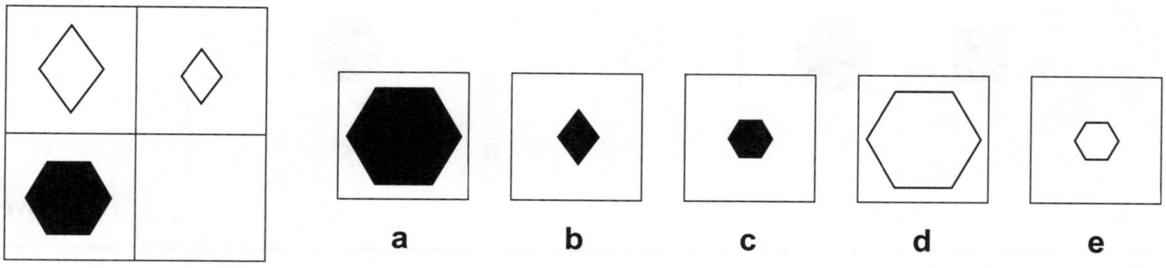

Answer: c

1

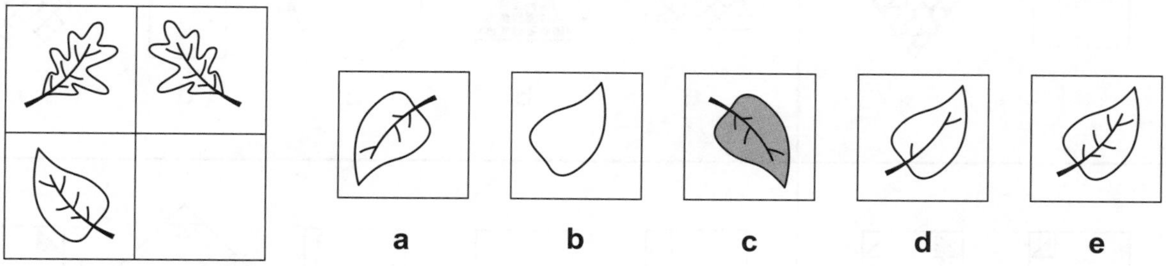

2

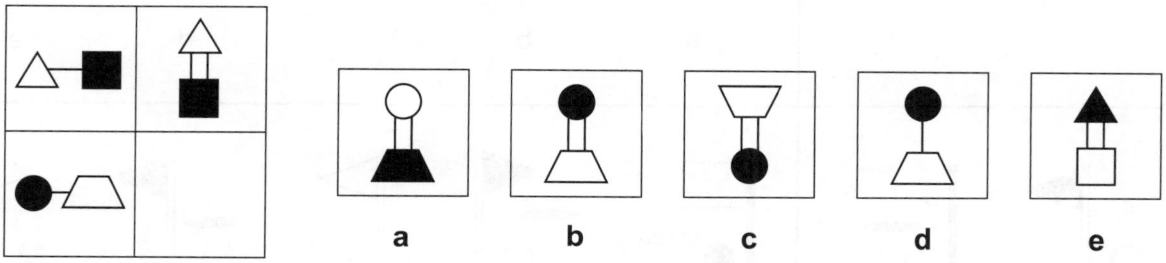

3

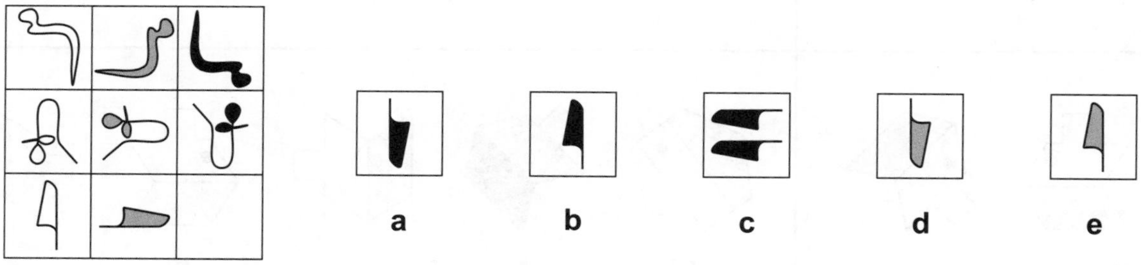

4

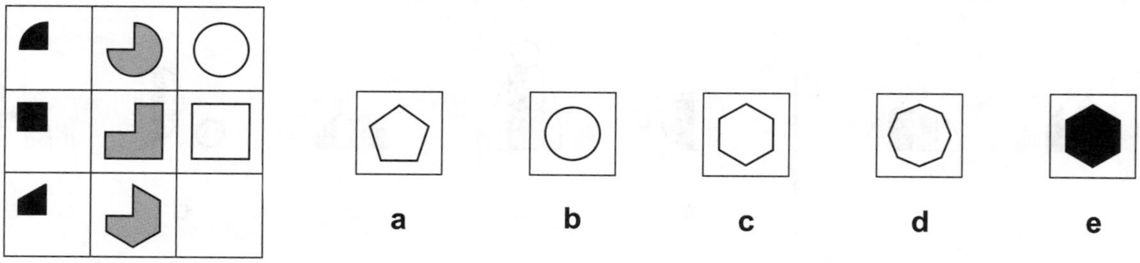

/ 4

Section 5 — Find the Figure Like the First Two

In each question, there are two figures on the left that are like each other in some way. Work out which of the five figures on the right is most like the two figures on the left.

Example:

a b c d e

Answer: c

(1)

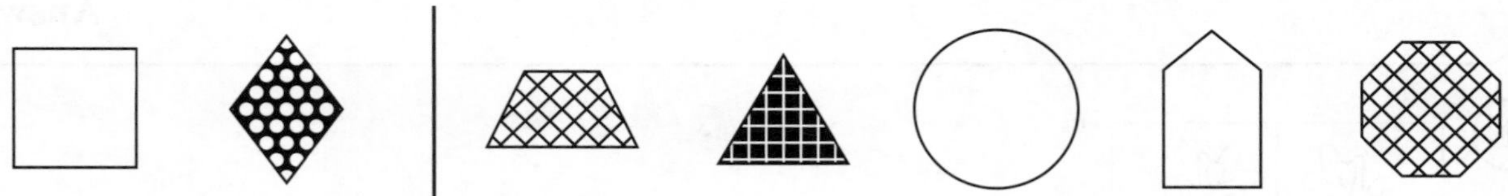

a b c d e

(2)

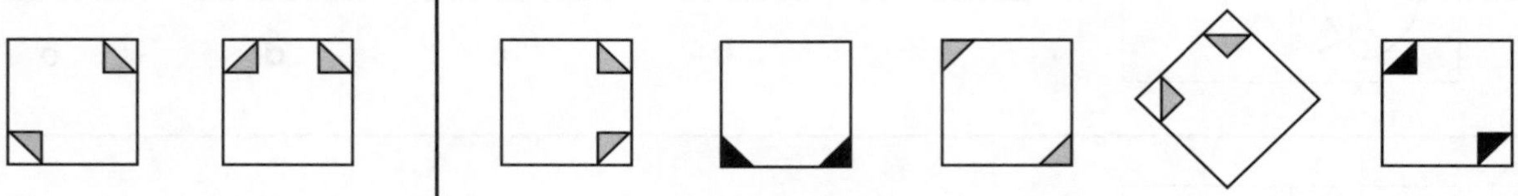

a b c d e

(3)

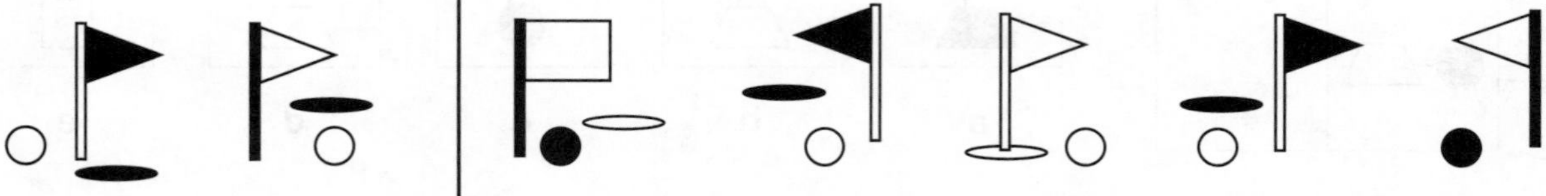

a b c d e

(4)

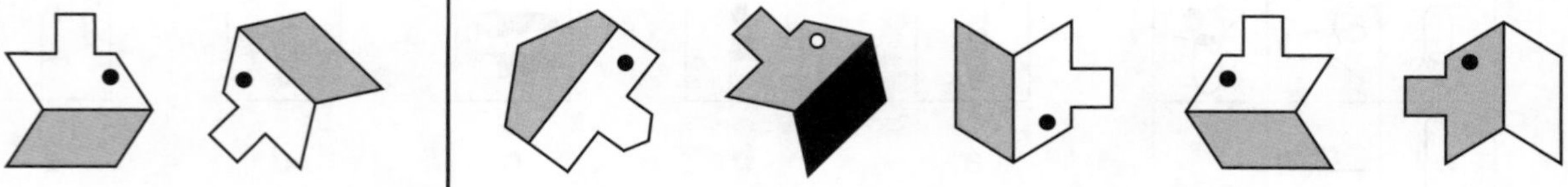

a b c d e

(5)

a b c d e

/ 5

Section 6 — Complete the Series

Each of these questions has five squares on the left that are arranged in order. One of the squares is empty. Work out which of the five squares on the right should replace the empty square.

Example:

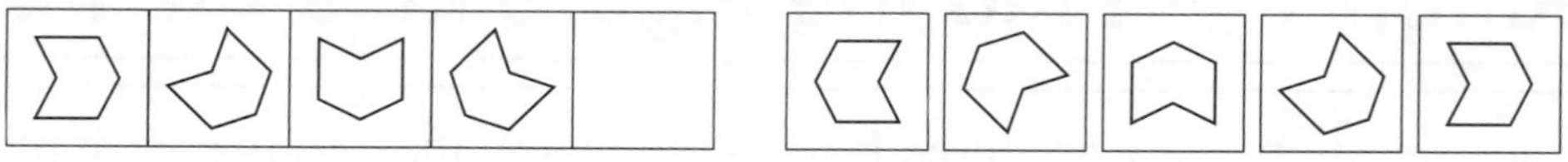

a b c d e

Answer: a

1

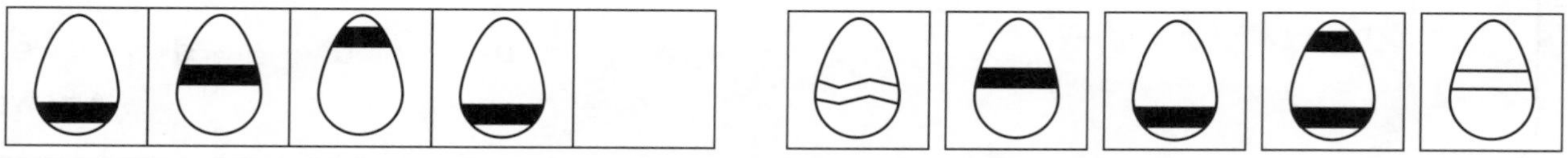

a b c d e

2

a b c d e

3

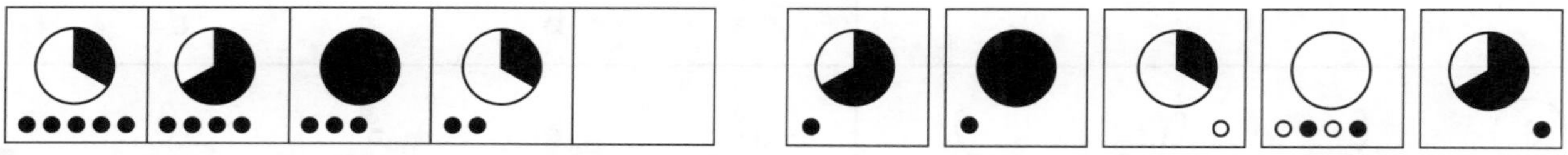

a b c d e

4

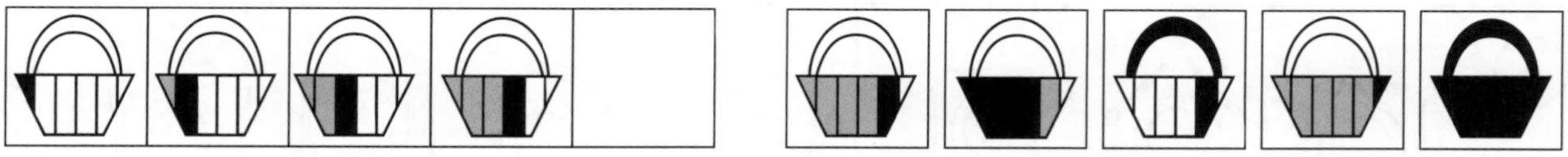

a b c d e

5

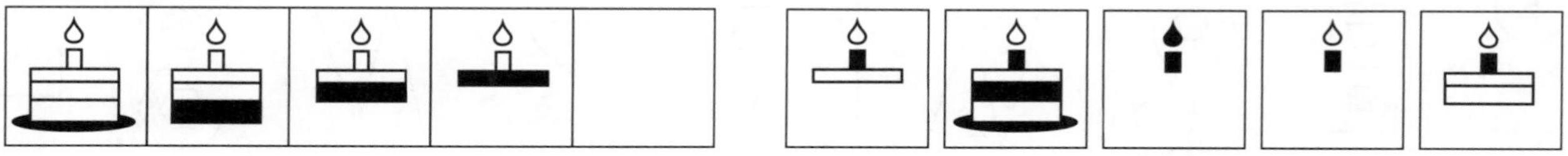

a b c d e

/ 5 Total / 28

Assessment Test 6

You can print **multiple-choice answer sheets** for these questions from our website — go to www.cgplearning.co.uk/11+. If you'd prefer to answer them in standard write-in format, just circle the letter underneath your answer. The test should take around 15 minutes.

Section 1 — Find the Figure Like the First Three

In each question, there are three figures on the left that are like each other in some way. Work out which of the five figures on the right is most like the three figures on the left.

Example:

a b c d e

Answer: c

1

a b c d e

2

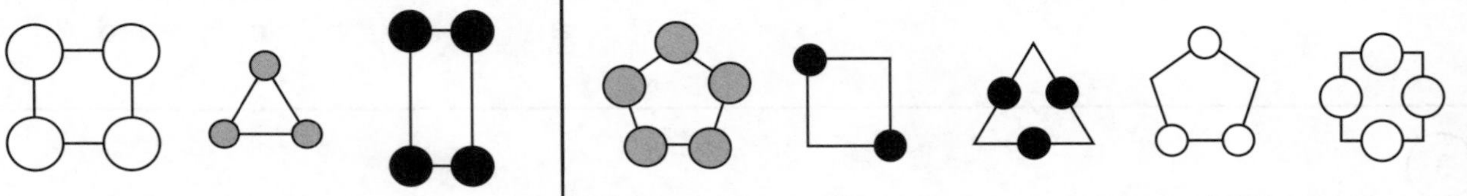

a b c d e

3

a b c d e

4

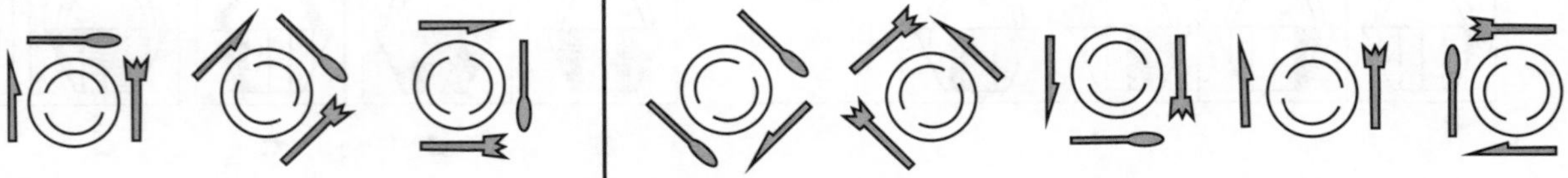

a b c d e

5

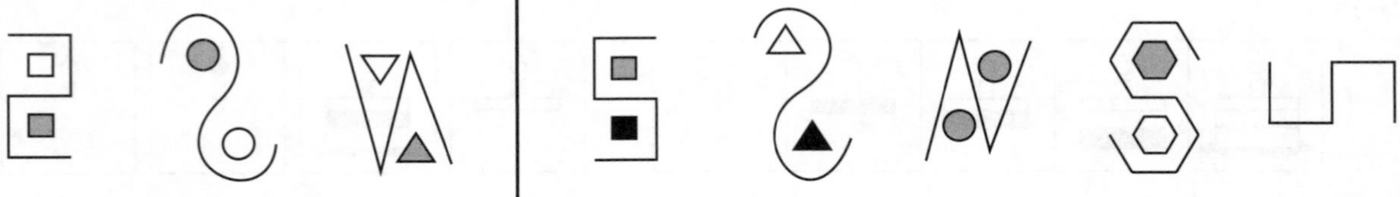

a b c d e

/ 5

Section 2 — Complete the Series

Each of these questions has five squares on the left that are arranged in order. One of the squares is empty. Work out which of the five squares on the right should replace the empty square.

Example:

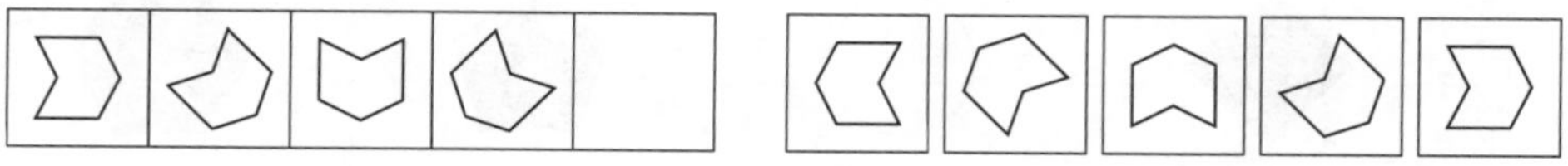

a b c d e

Answer: a

1

a b c d e

2

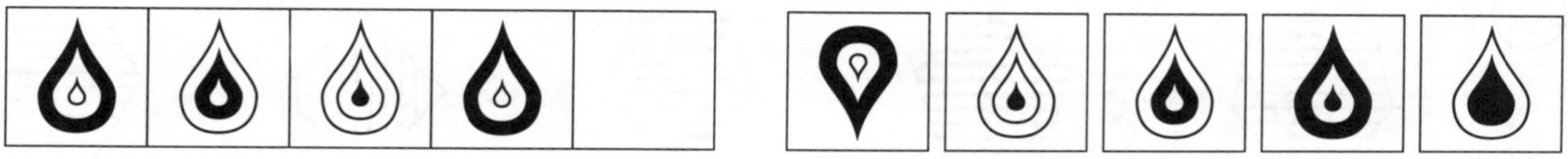

a b c d e

3

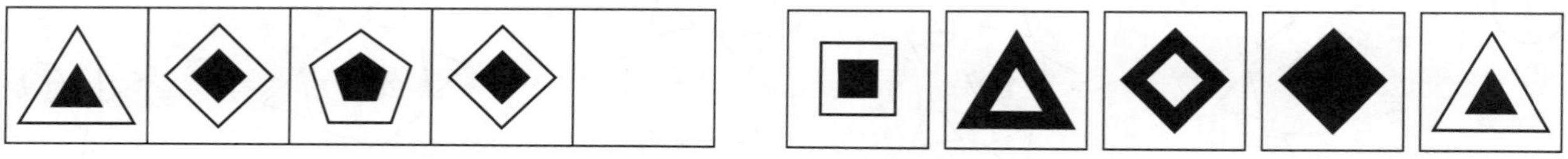

a b c d e

4

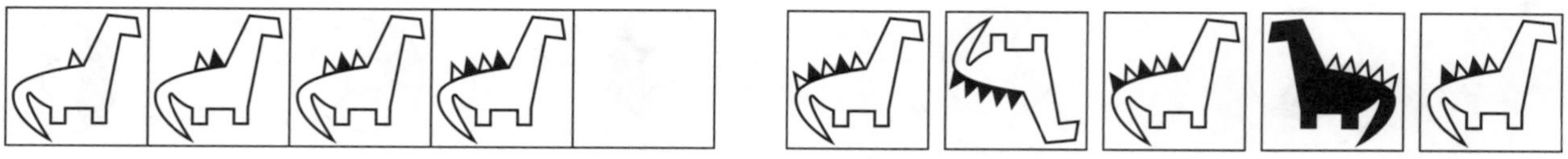

a b c d e

5

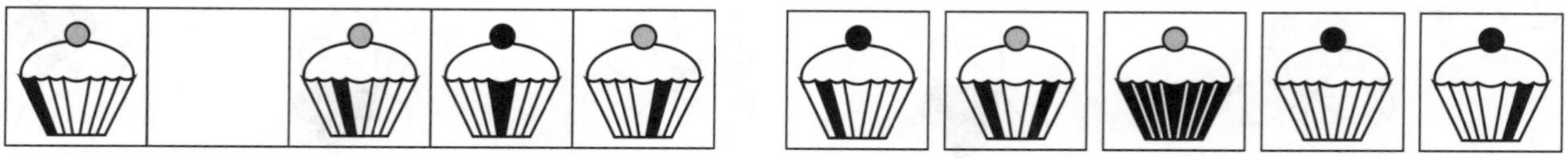

a b c d e

/ 5

Section 3 — Odd One Out

Each of the questions below has five figures.
Find the figure in each row that is most unlike the others.

Example:

a b c d e

Answer: b

1

a b c d e

2

a b c d e

3

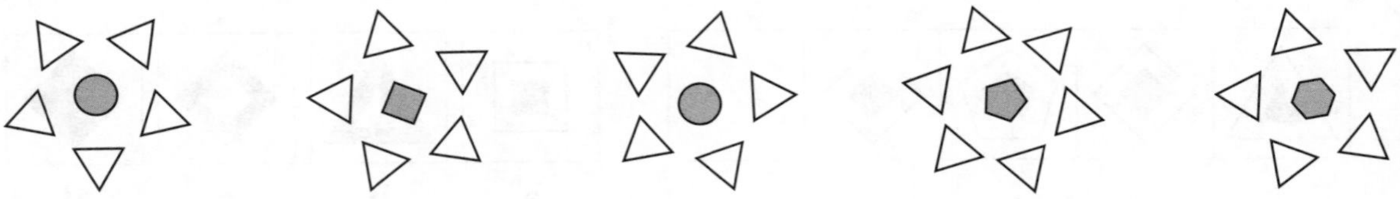

a b c d e

4

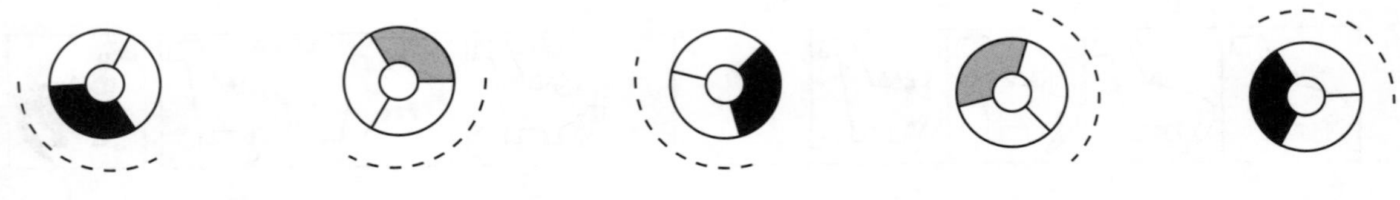

a b c d e

5

a b c d e

/ 5

Section 4 — Complete the Pair

The first figure in each question changes to become the second figure. Work out how the first figure has been changed. Then find the figure on the right that would match the third figure if it was changed in the same way.

Example:

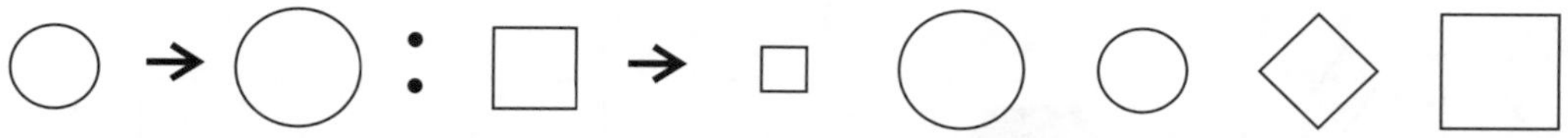

a b c d e

Answer: e

1

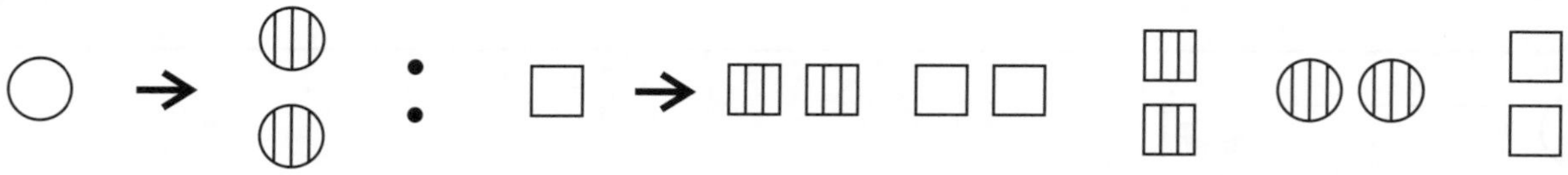

a b c d e

2

a b c d e

3

a b c d e

4

a b c d e

5

a b c d e

/ 5

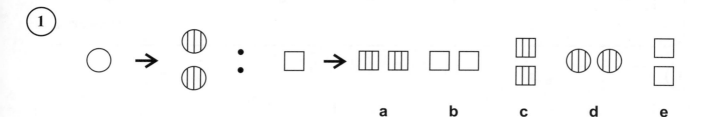

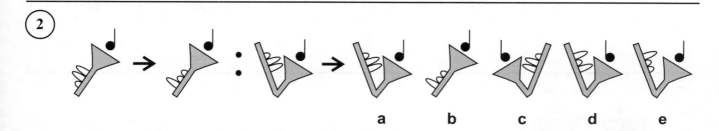

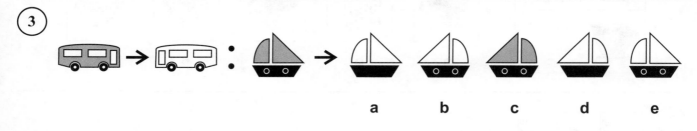

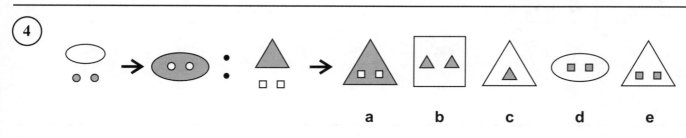

Section 5 — Complete the Grid

On the left of each question below is a grid with one empty square.
Work out which of the five squares on the right should replace the empty square.

Example:

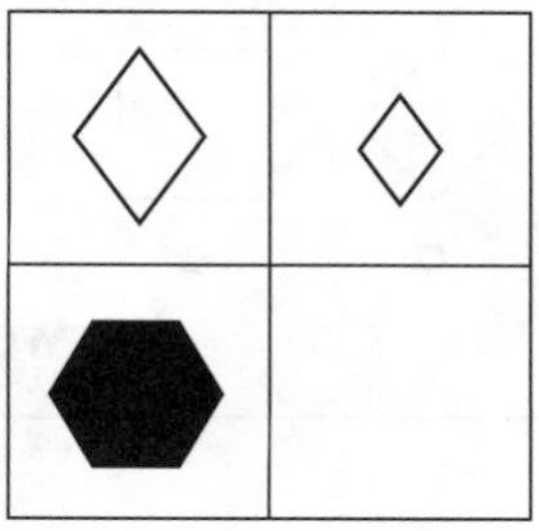

a b c d e

Answer: c

(1)

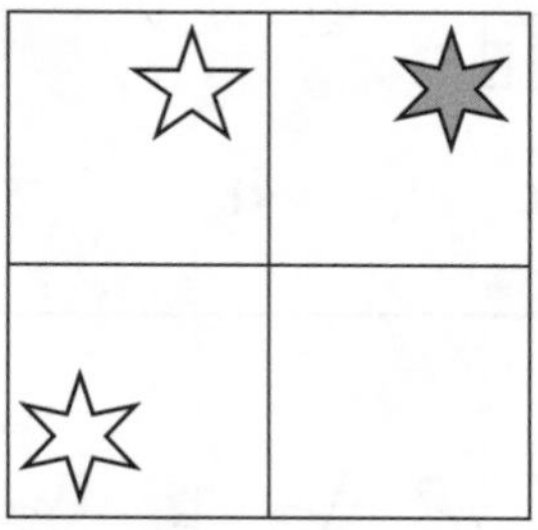

a b c d e

(2)

a b c d e

(3)

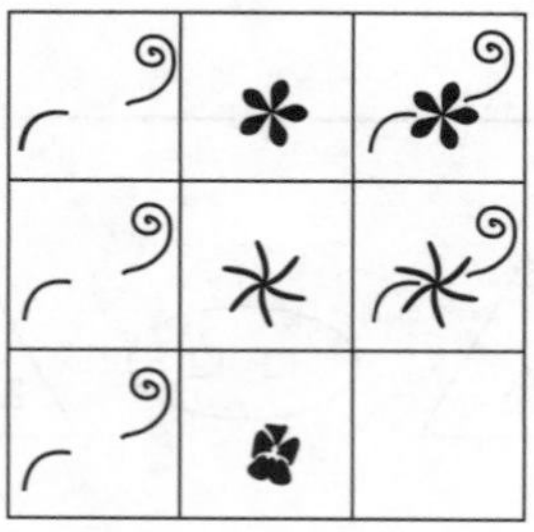

a b c d e

(4)

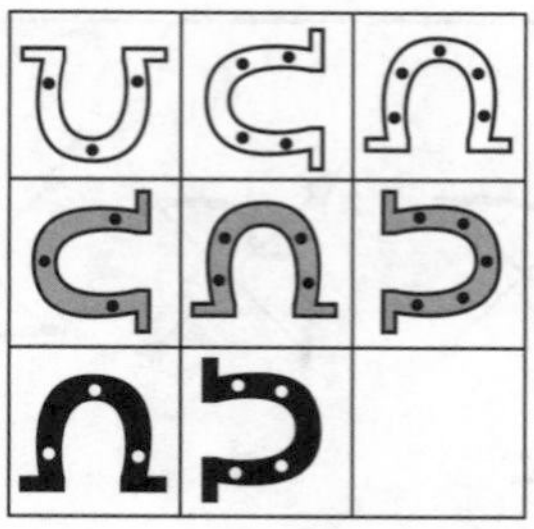

a b c d e

/ 4

Section 6 — Vertical Code

Each question has three figures on the left with code letters that describe them. You need to work out what the code letters mean. The figure on the right is missing its code. Work out which of the five codes on the right describes this figure.

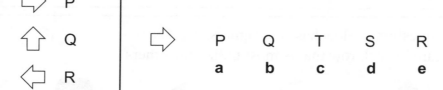

Example:

P
Q
R

P	Q	T	S	R
a	**b**	**c**	**d**	**e**

Answer: a

The arrow pointing right has the code letter P. The arrow pointing up has the code letter Q. The arrow pointing left has the code letter R. The figure on the right is an arrow pointing right, so its code must be P and the answer is **a**.

1

CM
DM
DN

CN	DM	CM	DP	DN
a	**b**	**c**	**d**	**e**

2

RA
SB
RB

SB	RB	SA	RA	RC
a	**b**	**c**	**d**	**e**

3

LP
NQ
MQ

NP	MP	LQ	LP	MQ
a	**b**	**c**	**d**	**e**

4

XF
YG
XE

XF	YE	XG	YG	YF
a	**b**	**c**	**d**	**e**

/ 4 Total / 28

END OF TEST

Assessment Test 7

You can print **multiple-choice answer sheets** for these questions from our website — go to www.cgplearning.co.uk/11+. If you'd prefer to answer them in standard write-in format, just circle the letter underneath your answer. The test should take around 15 minutes.

Section 1 — Odd One Out

Each of the questions below has five figures.
Find the figure in each row that is most unlike the others.

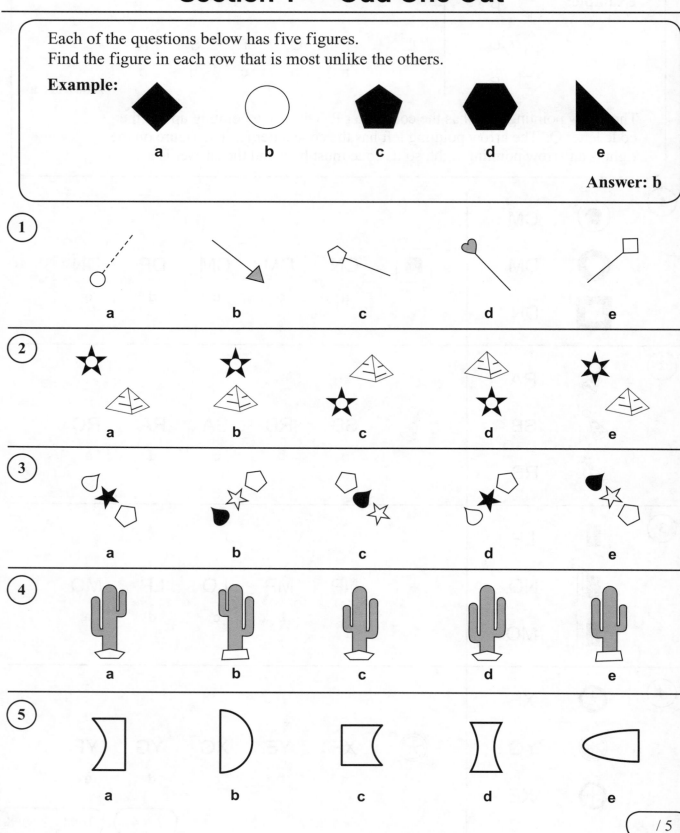

Example:

a b c d e

Answer: b

1

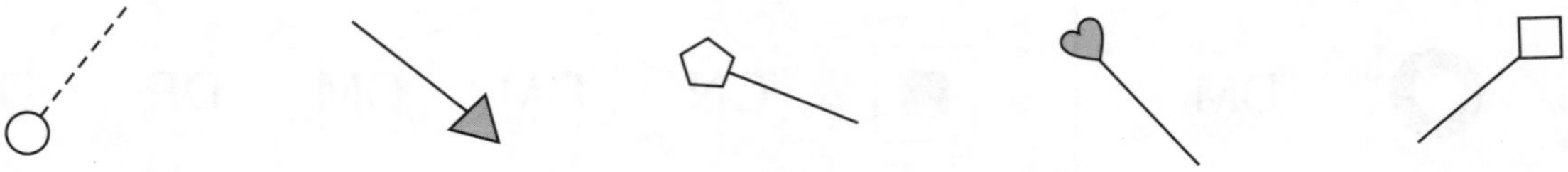

a b c d e

2

a b c d e

3

a b c d e

4

a b c d e

5

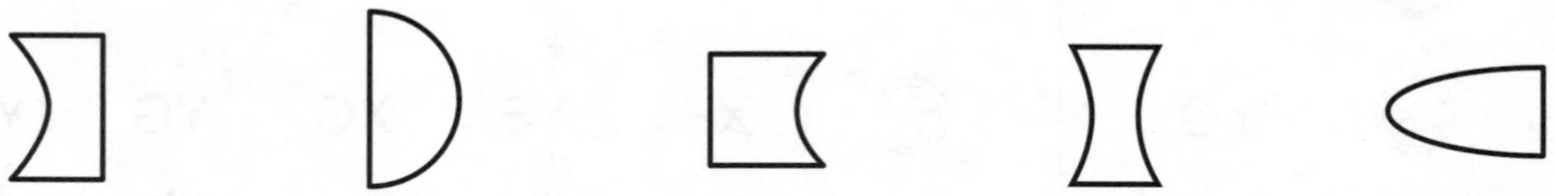

a b c d e

/ 5

Section 2 — Complete the Grid

On the left of each question below is a grid with one empty square.
Work out which of the five squares on the right should replace the empty square.

Example:

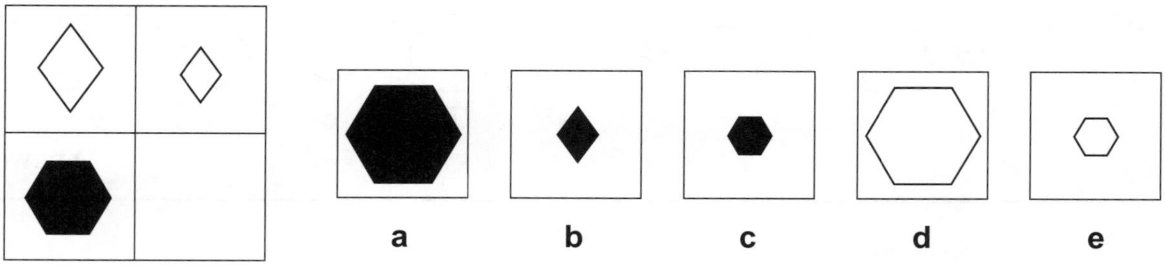

a b c d e

Answer: c

(1)

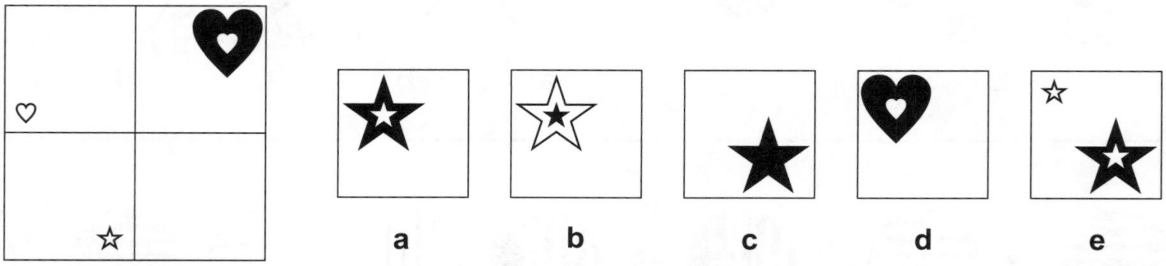

a b c d e

(2)

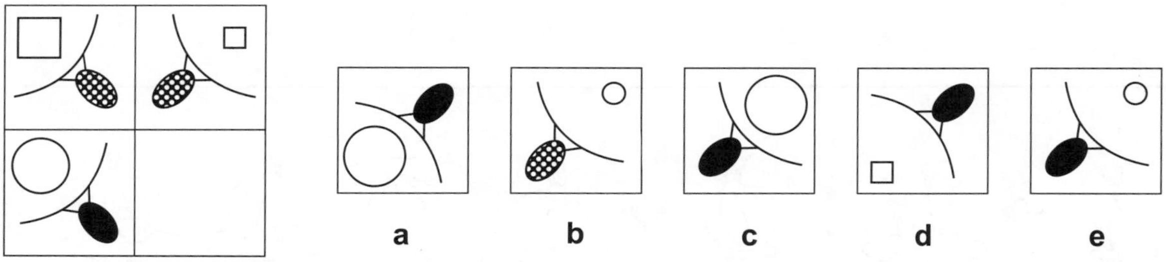

a b c d e

(3)

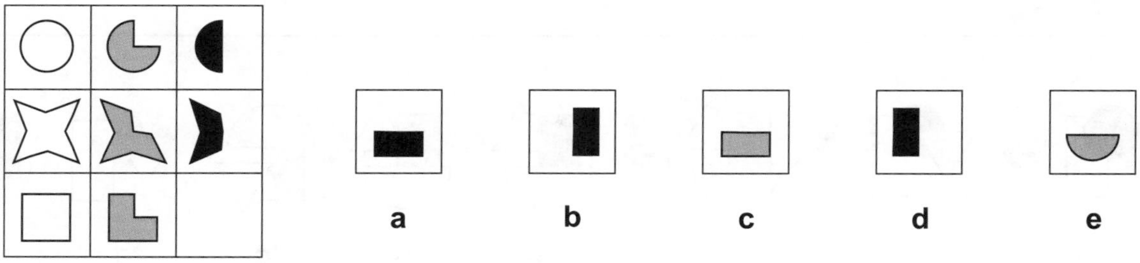

a b c d e

(4)

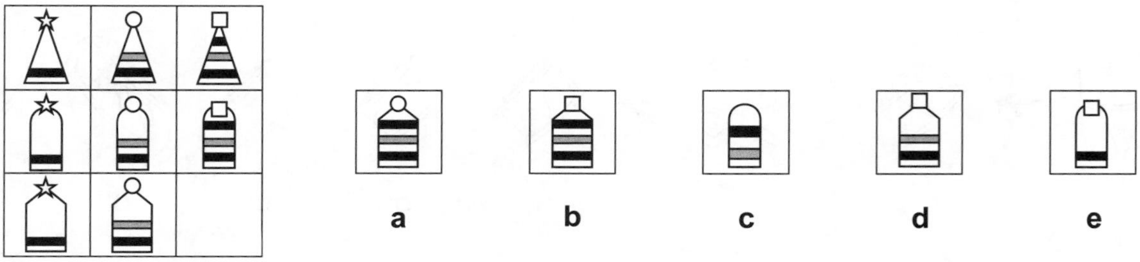

a b c d e

/ 4

Section 3 — Complete the Pair

The first figure in each question changes to become the second figure. Work out how the first figure has been changed. Then find the figure on the right that would match the third figure if it was changed in the same way.

Example:

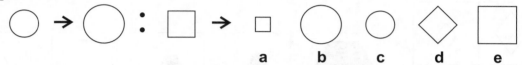

a b c d e

Answer: e

(1)

a b c d e

(2)

a b c d e

(3)

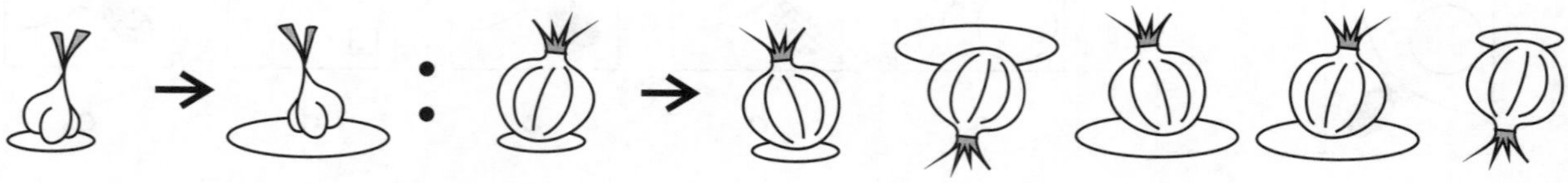

a b c d e

(4)

a b c d e

(5)

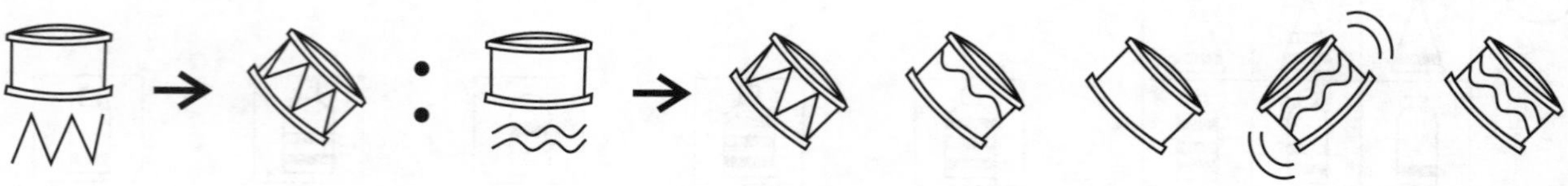

a b c d e

/ 5

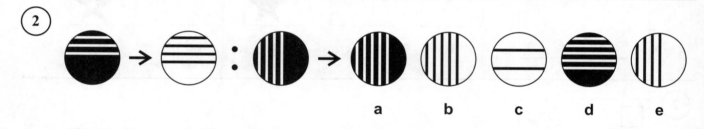

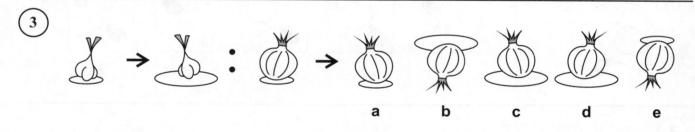

Section 4 — Vertical Code

Each question has three figures on the left with code letters that describe them. You need to work out what the code letters mean. The figure on the right is missing its code. Work out which of the five codes on the right describes this figure.

Example:

P

Q

R

P	Q	T	S	R
a	**b**	**c**	**d**	**e**

Answer: a

The arrow pointing right has the code letter P. The arrow pointing up has the code letter Q. The arrow pointing left has the code letter R. The figure on the right is an arrow pointing right, so its code must be P and the answer is **a**.

1.

AX

BY

BX

AX	BZ	AY	BX	BY
a	**b**	**c**	**d**	**e**

2.

FP

GP

GQ

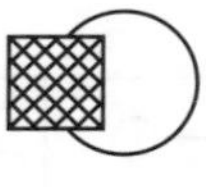

GQ	FQ	GP	FP	GR
a	**b**	**c**	**d**	**e**

3.

ZS

XS

YT

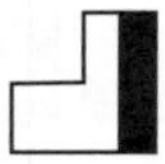

XS	ZS	YS	XT	ZT
a	**b**	**c**	**d**	**e**

4.

VE

VD

WC

VC	WE	VD	WD	WC
a	**b**	**c**	**d**	**e**

/ 4

Section 5 — Complete the Series

Each of these questions has five squares on the left that are arranged in order. One of the squares is empty. Work out which of the five squares on the right should replace the empty square.

Example:

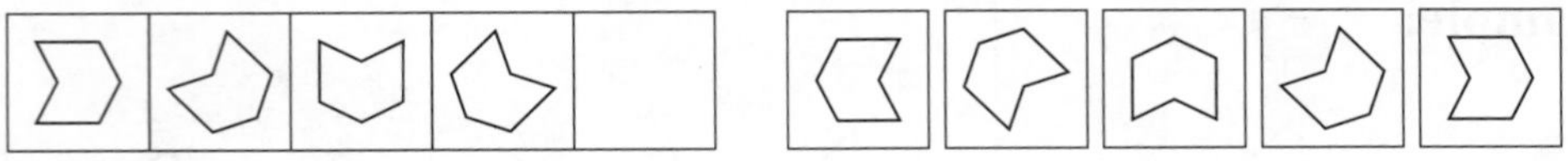

a b c d e

Answer: a

1

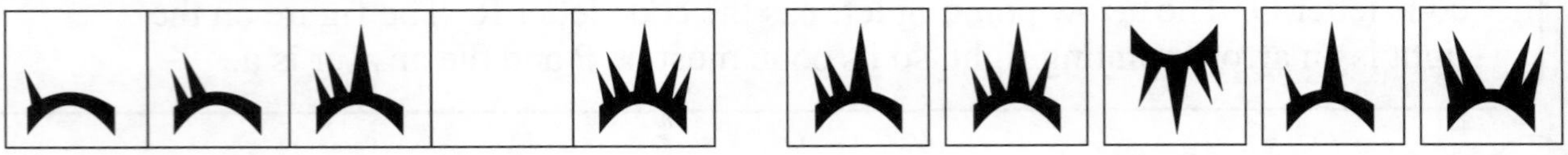

a b c d e

2

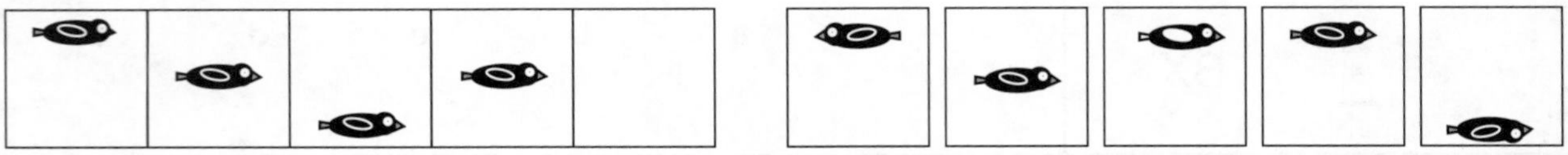

a b c d e

3

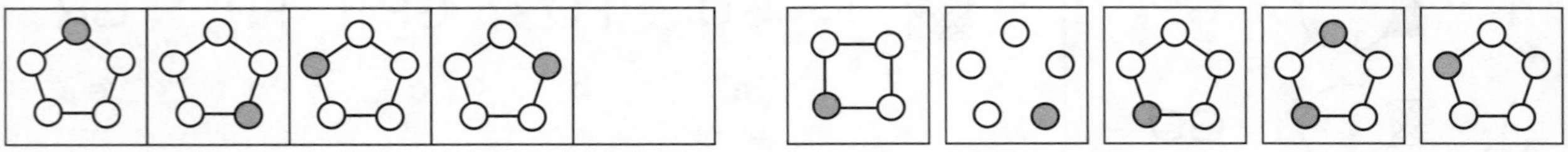

a b c d e

4

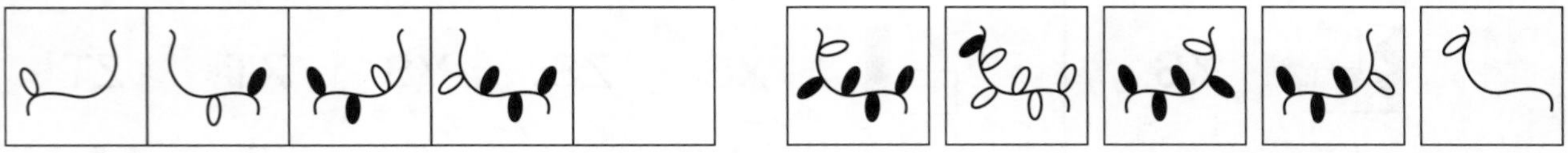

a b c d e

5

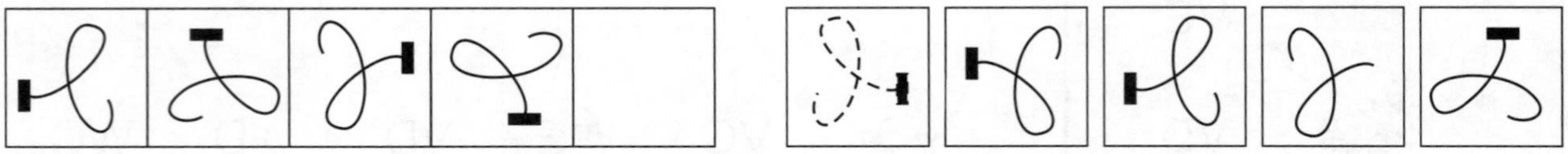

a b c d e

/ 5

Section 6 — Find the Figure Like the First Two

In each question, there are two figures on the left that are like each other in some way. Work out which of the five figures on the right is most like the two figures on the left.

Example:

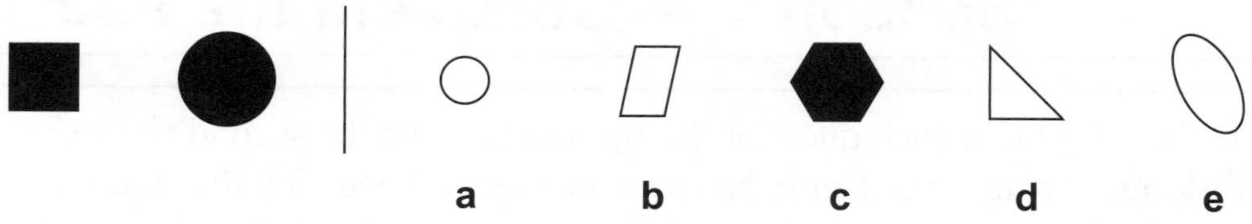

Answer: c

1

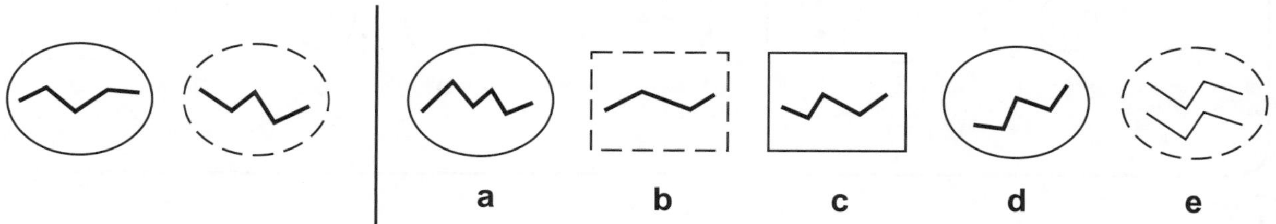

2

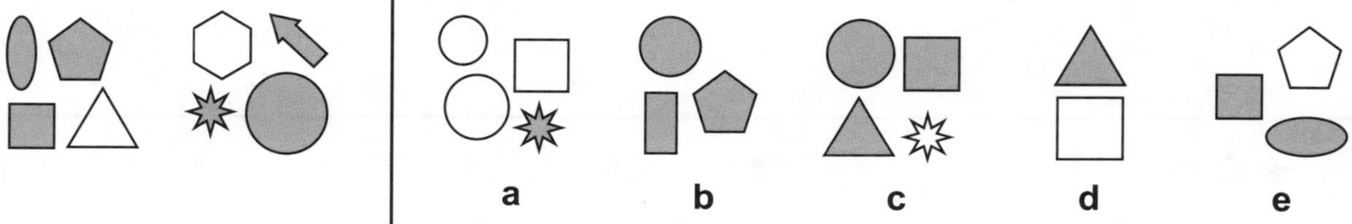

3

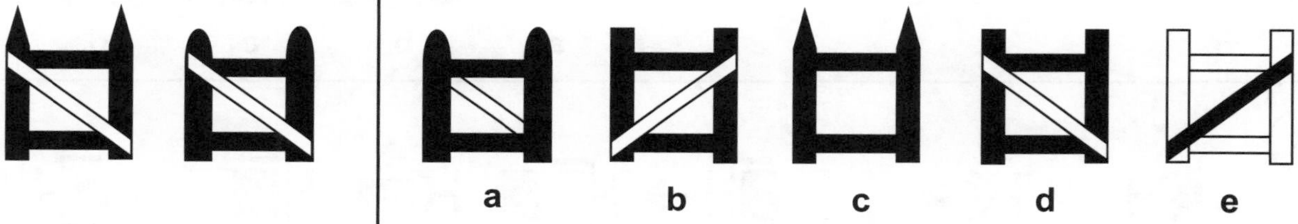

4

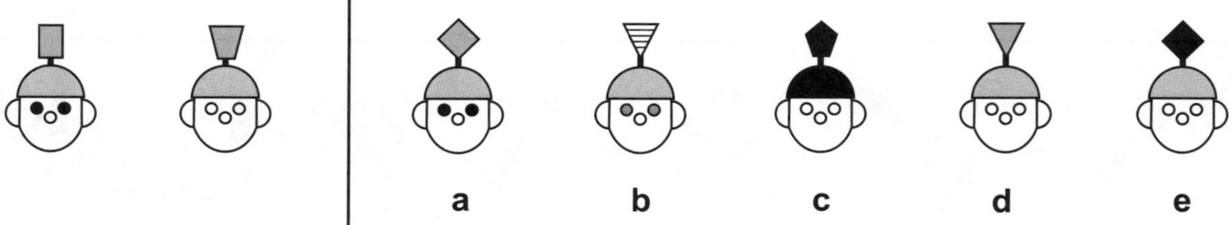

5

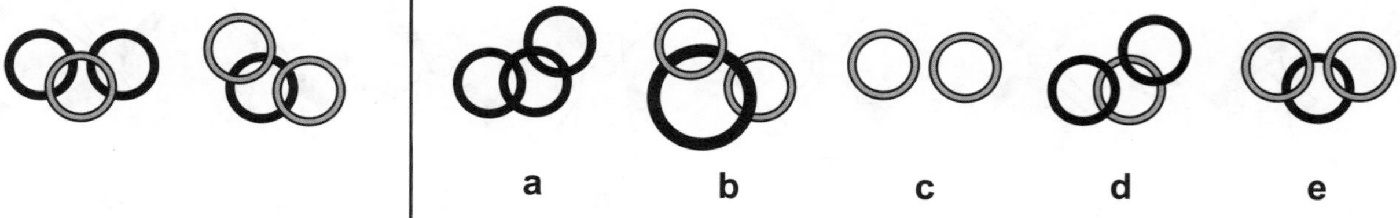

/ 5   Total / 28

END OF TEST

Assessment Test 8

You can print **multiple-choice answer sheets** for these questions from our website — go to www.cgplearning.co.uk/11+. If you'd prefer to answer them in standard write-in format, just circle the letter underneath your answer. The test should take around 15 minutes.

Section 1 — Complete the Pair

The first figure in each question changes to become the second figure. Work out how the first figure has been changed. Then find the figure on the right that would match the third figure if it was changed in the same way.

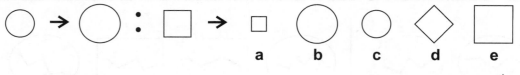

Example:

a b c d e

Answer: e

1

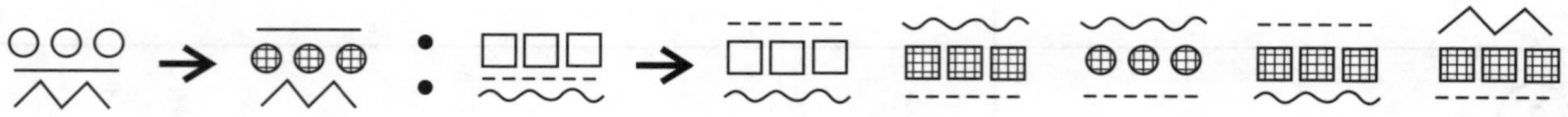

a b c d e

2

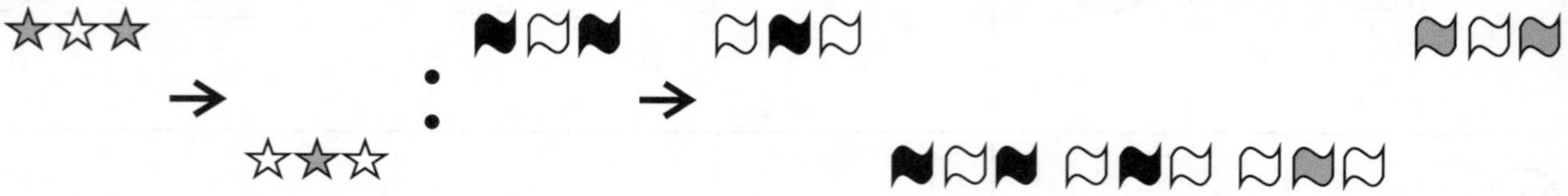

a b c d e

3

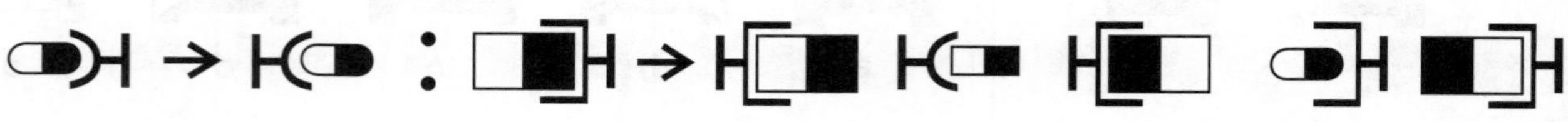

a b c d e

4

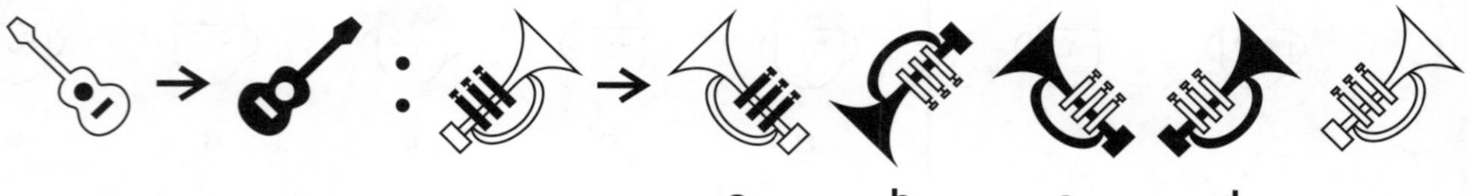

a b c d e

5

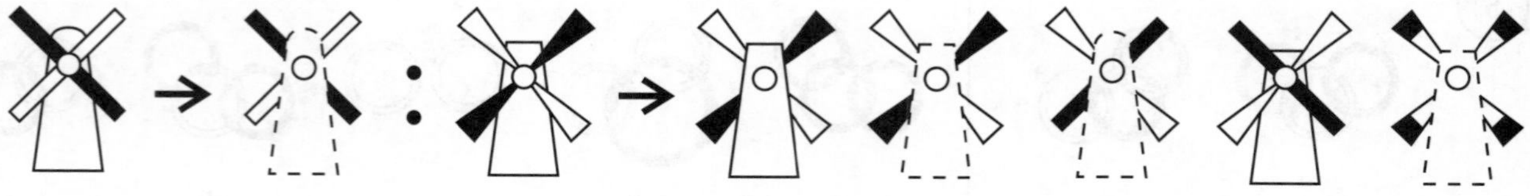

a b c d e

/ 5

Section 2 — Vertical Code

Each question has three figures on the left with code letters that describe them. You need to work out what the code letters mean. The figure on the right is missing its code. Work out which of the five codes on the right describes this figure.

Example:

P

Q

R

P	Q	T	S	R
a	**b**	**c**	**d**	**e**

Answer: a

The arrow pointing right has the code letter P. The arrow pointing up has the code letter Q. The arrow pointing left has the code letter R. The figure on the right is an arrow pointing right, so its code must be P and the answer is **a**.

1

BF

CF

CG

BG	CG	CF	BE	BF
a	**b**	**c**	**d**	**e**

2

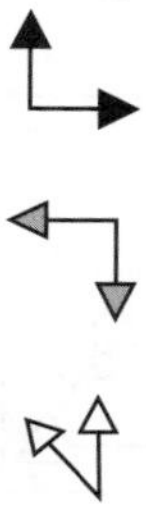

XP

YP

ZQ

YQ	ZP	XQ	XP	YP
a	**b**	**c**	**d**	**e**

3

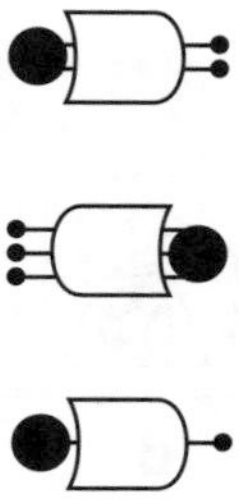

LR

NS

MR

LS	MS	MR	NR	NS
a	**b**	**c**	**d**	**e**

4

PT

RS

RT

RS	PT	PR	PS	RT
a	**b**	**c**	**d**	**e**

/ 4

Section 3 — Complete the Series

Each of these questions has five squares on the left that are arranged in order. One of the squares is empty. Work out which of the five squares on the right should replace the empty square.

Example:

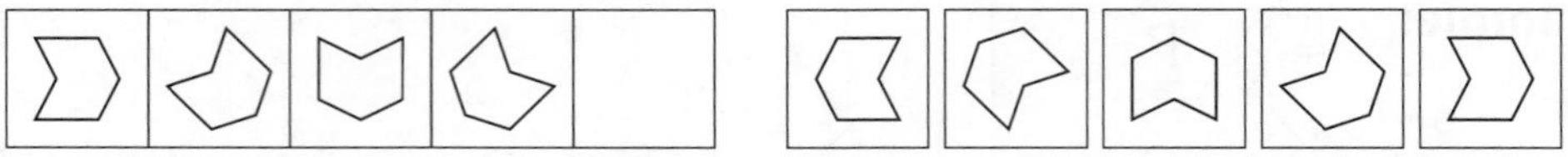

a b c d e

Answer: a

(1)

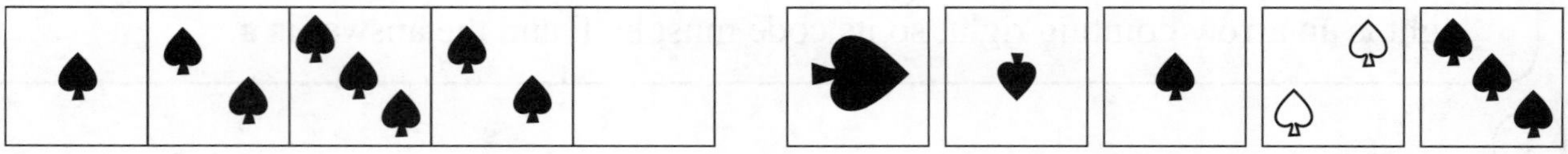

a b c d e

(2)

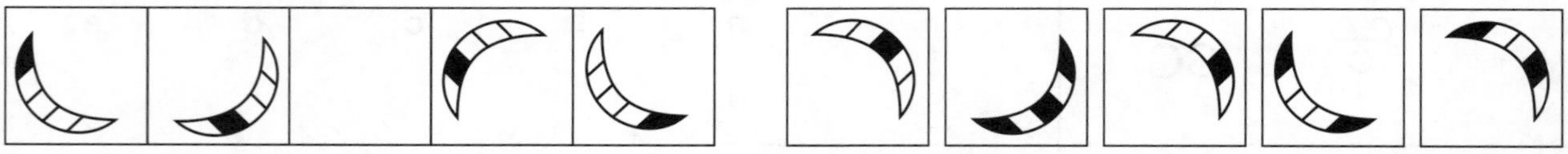

a b c d e

(3)

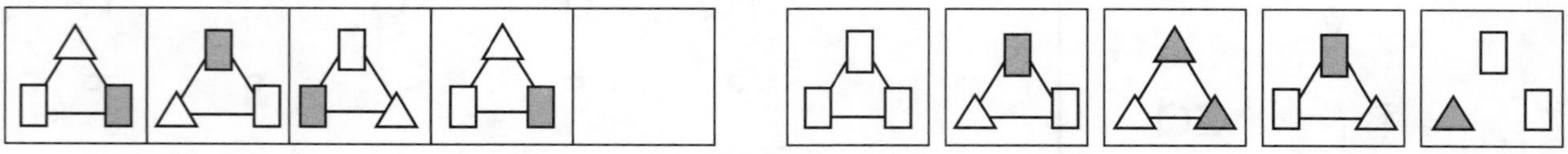

a b c d e

(4)

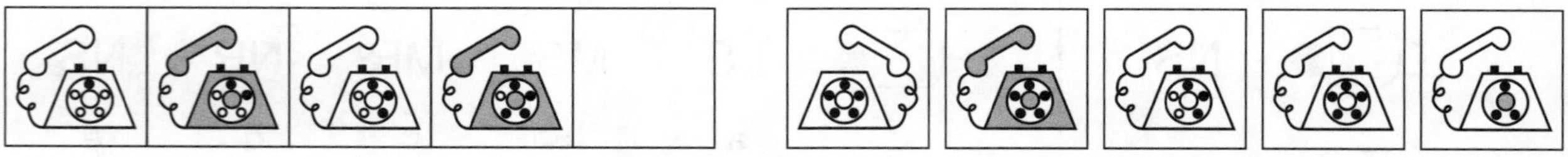

a b c d e

(5)

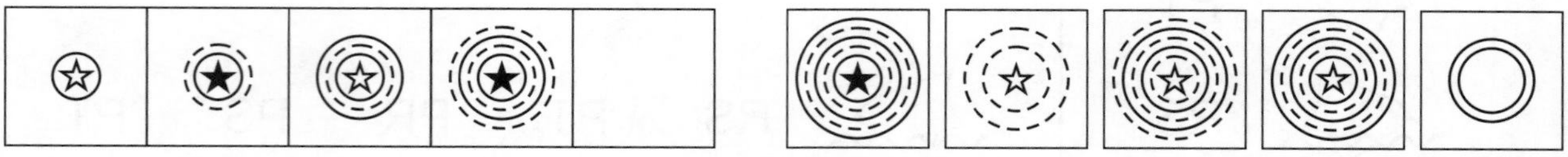

a b c d e

/ 5

Section 4 — Complete the Grid

On the left of each question below is a grid with one empty square.
Work out which of the five squares on the right should replace the empty square.

Example:

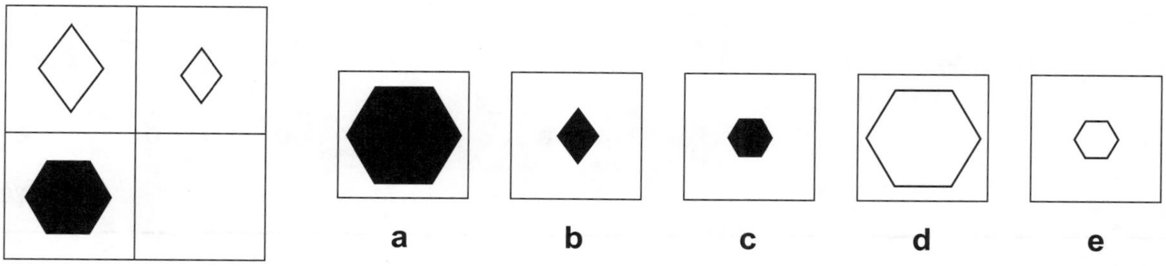

a b c d e

Answer: c

(1)

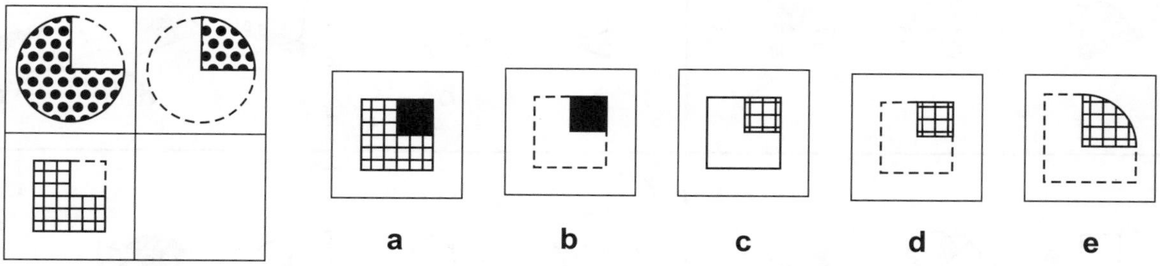

a b c d e

(2)

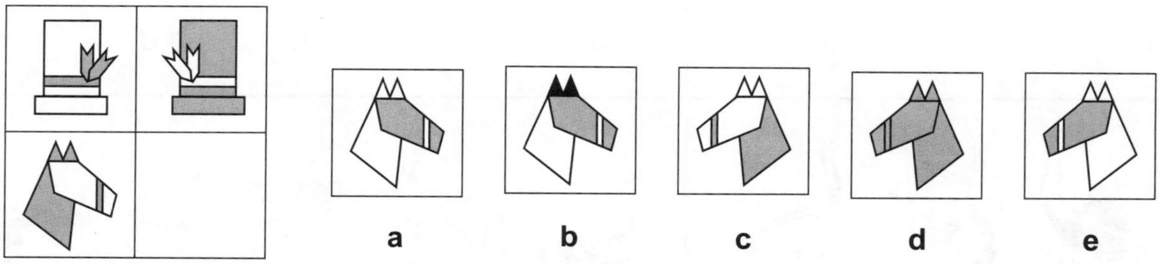

a b c d e

(3)

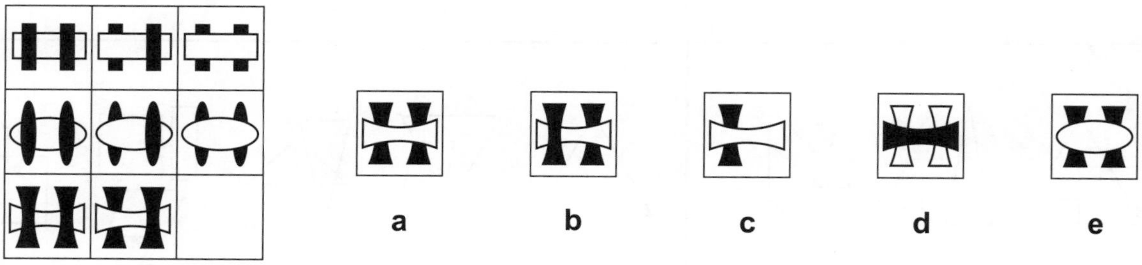

a b c d e

(4)

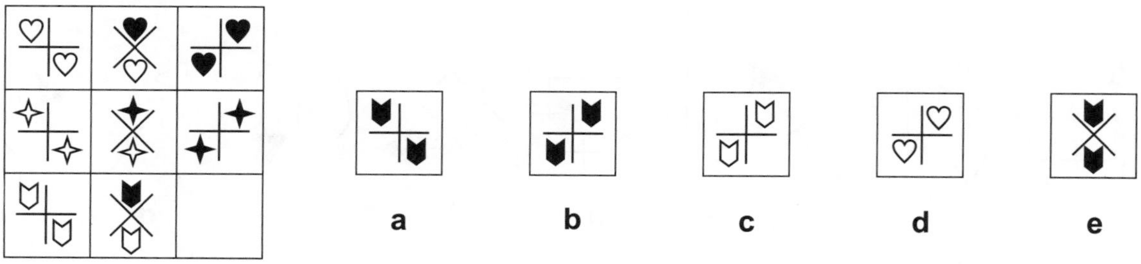

a b c d e

/ 4

Section 5 — Find the Figure Like the First Three

In each question, there are three figures on the left that are like each other in some way. Work out which of the five figures on the right is most like the three figures on the left.

Example:

a b c d e

Answer: c

(1)

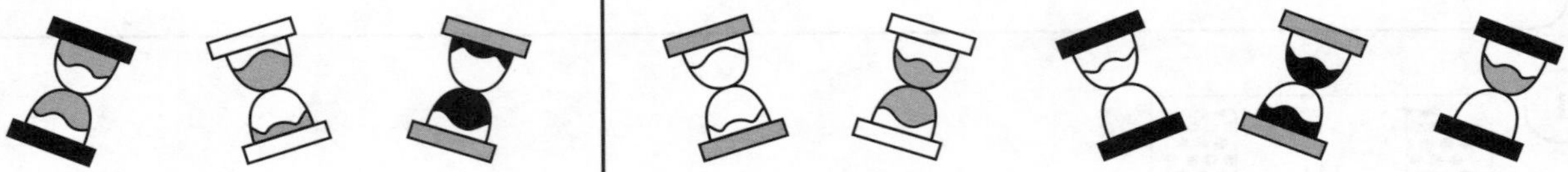

a b c d e

(2)

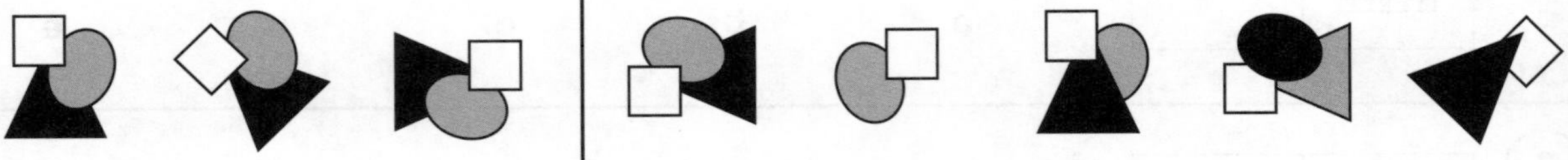

a b c d e

(3)

a b c d e

(4)

a b c d e

(5)

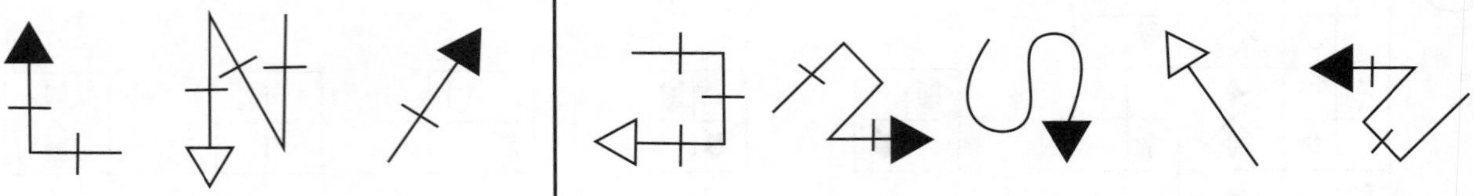

a b c d e

/ 5

Section 6 — Odd One Out

Each of the questions below has five figures.
Find the figure in each row that is most unlike the others.

Example:

a b c d e

Answer: b

(1)

a b c d e

(2)

a b c d e

(3)

a b c d e

(4)

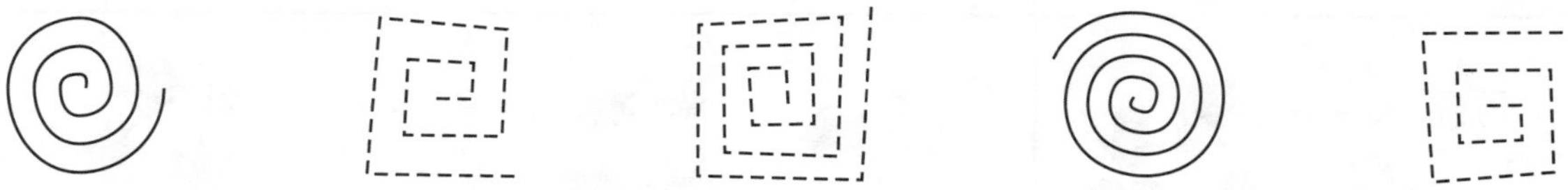

a b c d e

(5)

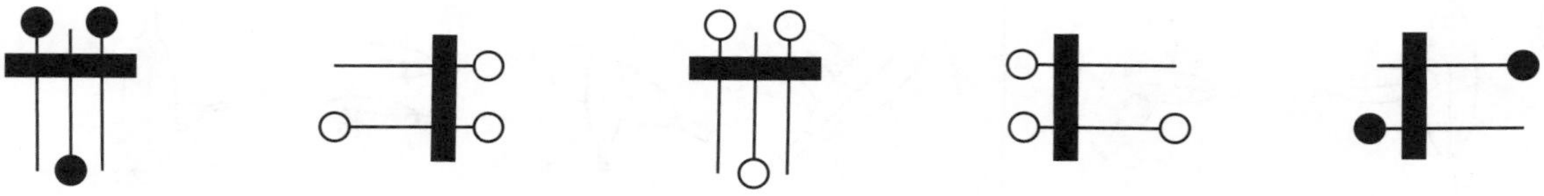

a b c d e

/ 5 Total / 28

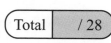

Assessment Test 9

You can print **multiple-choice answer sheets** for these questions from our website — go to www.cgplearning.co.uk/11+. If you'd prefer to answer them in standard write-in format, just circle the letter underneath your answer. The test should take around 15 minutes.

Section 1 — Find the Figure Like the First Two

In each question, there are two figures on the left that are like each other in some way. Work out which of the five figures on the right is most like the two figures on the left.

Example:

a b c d e

Answer: c

(1)

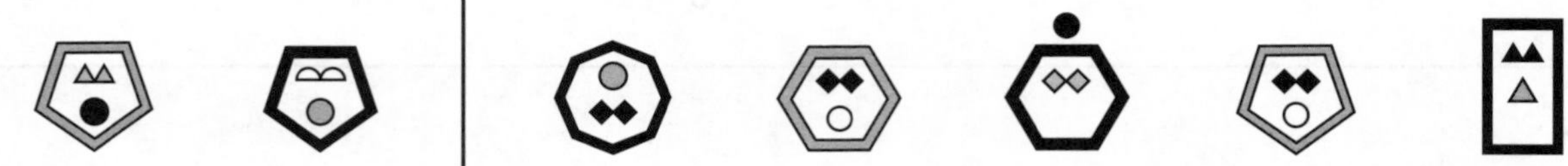

a b c d e

(2)

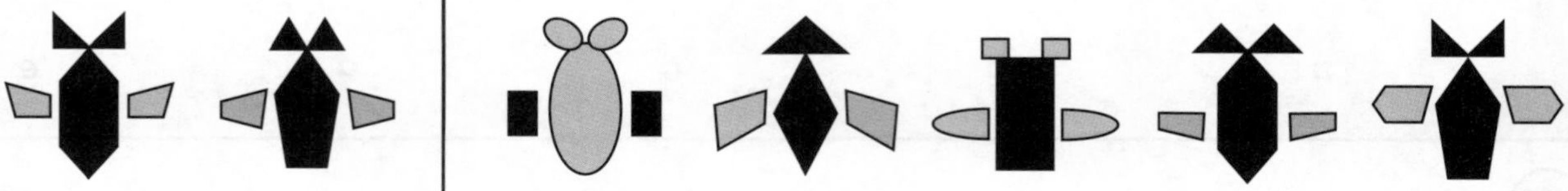

a b c d e

(3)

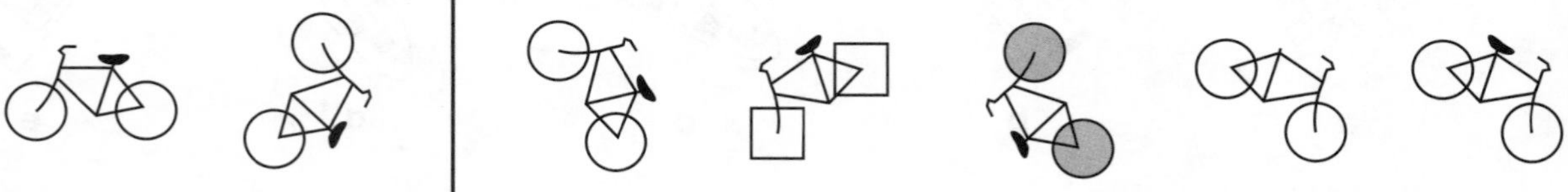

a b c d e

(4)

a b c d e

(5)

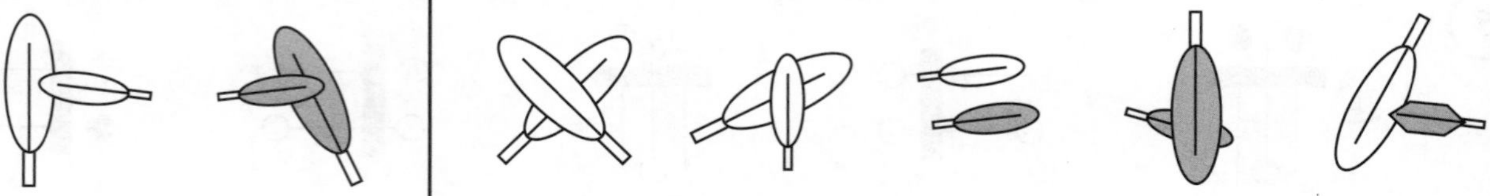

a b c d e

/ 5

Section 2 — Odd One Out

Each of the questions below has five figures.
Find the figure in each row that is most unlike the others.

Example:

a b c d e

Answer: b

(1)

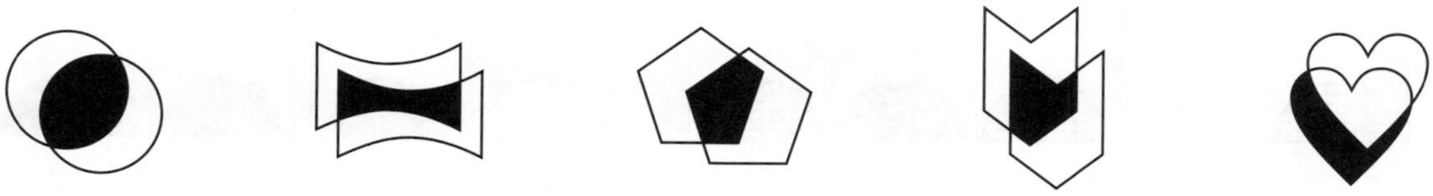

a b c d e

(2)

a b c d e

(3)

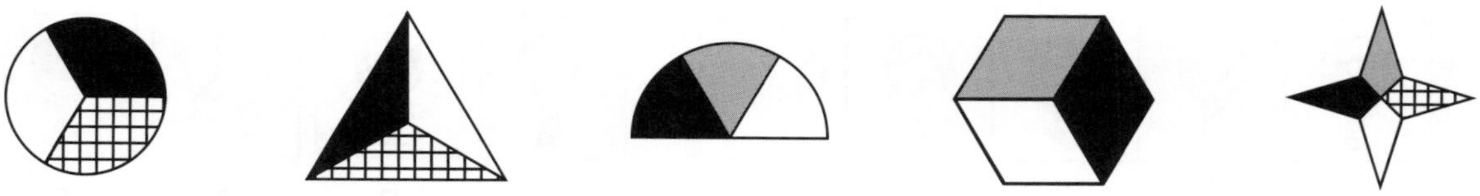

a b c d e

(4)

a b c d e

(5)

a b c d e

/ 5

Section 3 — Complete the Series

Each of these questions has five squares on the left that are arranged in order. One of the squares is empty. Work out which of the five squares on the right should replace the empty square.

Example:

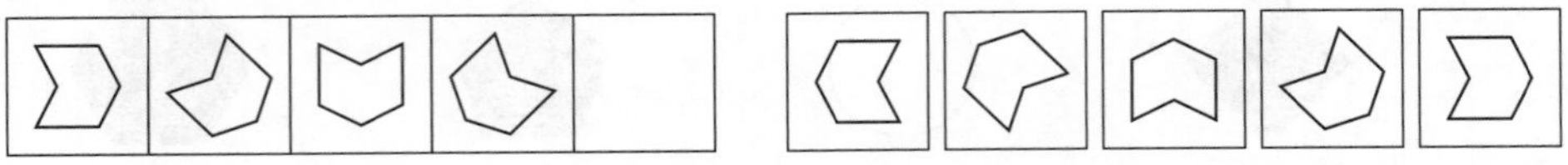

a b c d e

Answer: a

(1)

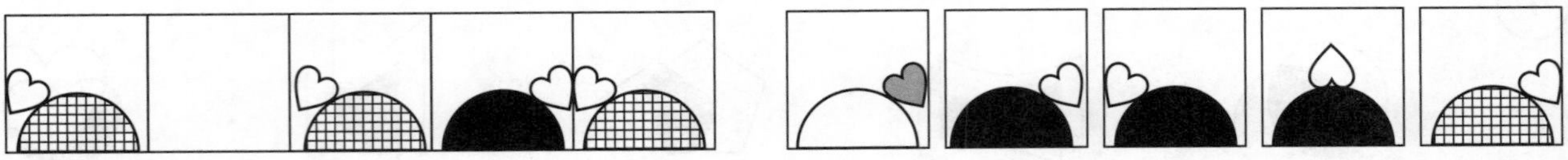

a b c d e

(2)

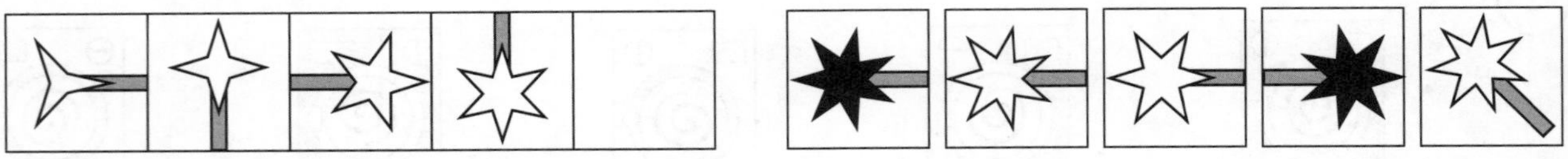

a b c d e

(3)

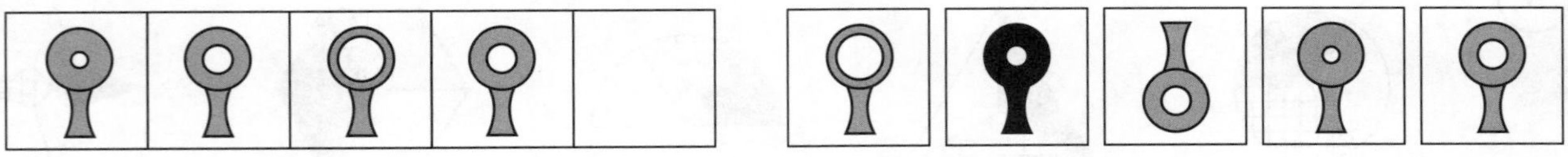

a b c d e

(4)

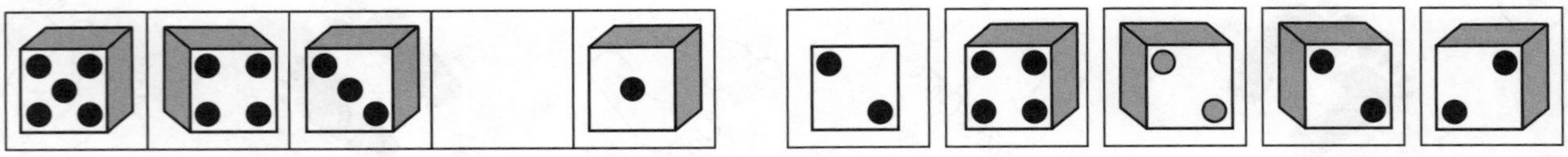

a b c d e

(5)

a b c d e

/ 5

Section 4 — Complete the Pair

The first figure in each question changes to become the second figure. Work out how the first figure has been changed. Then find the figure on the right that would match the third figure if it was changed in the same way.

Example:

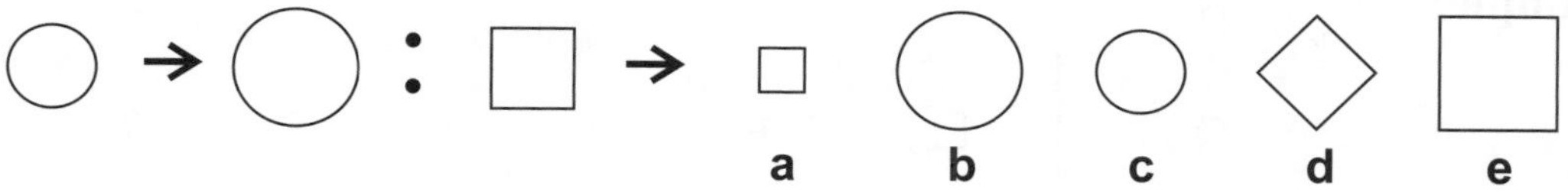

Answer: e

1

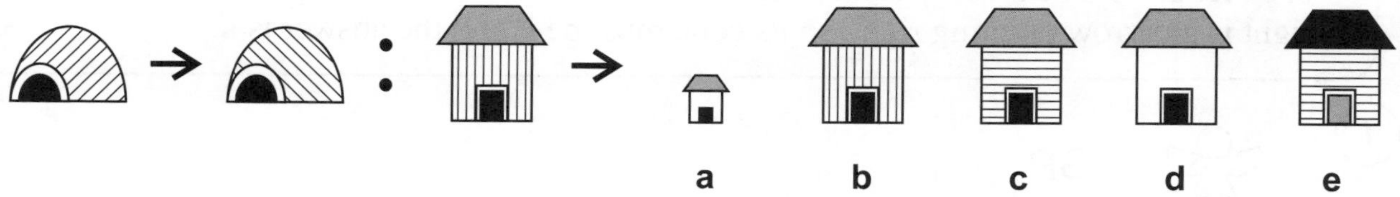

2

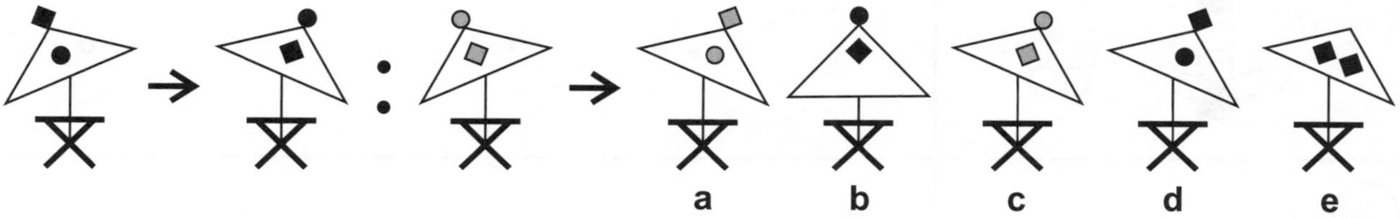

3

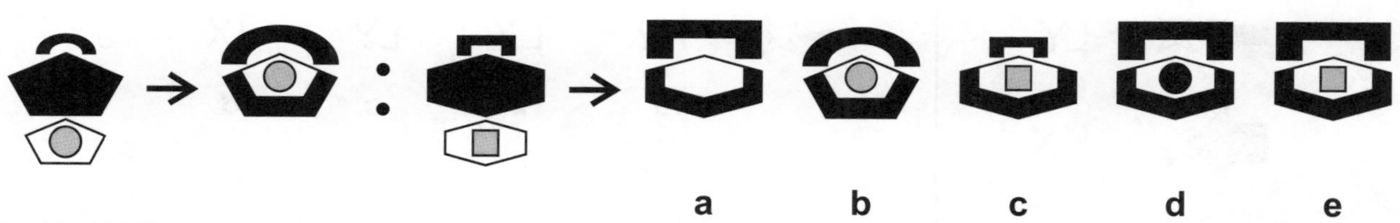

4

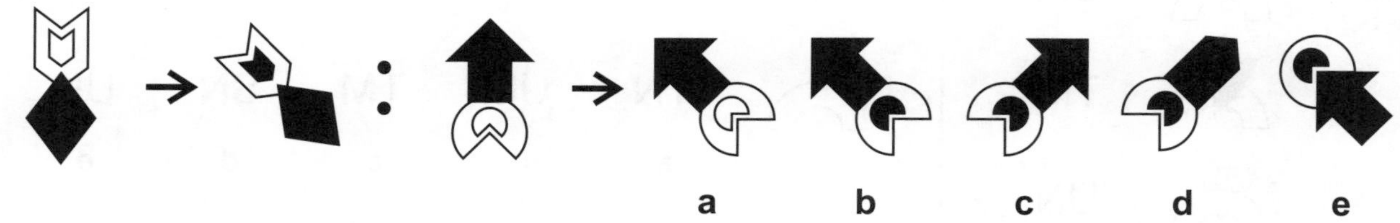

5

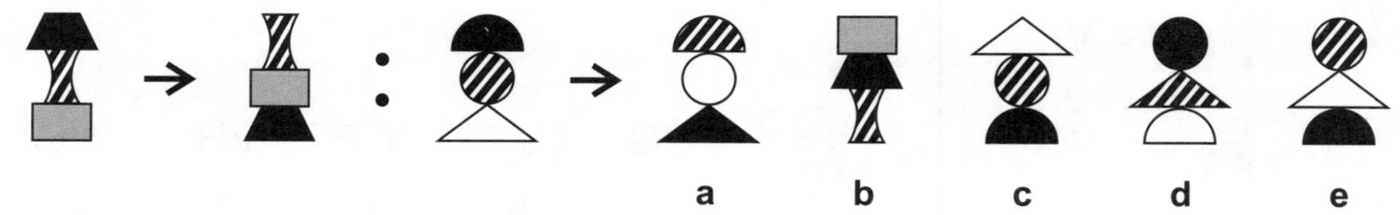

/ 5

Section 5 — Vertical Code

Each question has three figures on the left with code letters that describe them. You need to work out what the code letters mean. The figure on the right is missing its code. Work out which of the five codes on the right describes this figure.

Example:

P
Q
R

P	Q	T	S	R
a	**b**	**c**	**d**	**e**

Answer: a

The arrow pointing right has the code letter P. The arrow pointing up has the code letter Q. The arrow pointing left has the code letter R. The figure on the right is an arrow pointing right, so its code must be P and the answer is **a**.

1

GP
FQ
GQ

GR	FP	FQ	GQ	GP
a	**b**	**c**	**d**	**e**

2

JX
LY
KX

KY	LX	LY	JX	JY
a	**b**	**c**	**d**	**e**

3

SM
TM
UN

TN	UM	TM	SN	UN
a	**b**	**c**	**d**	**e**

4

VF
VG
WH

VG	VF	WF	VH	WG
a	**b**	**c**	**d**	**e**

/ 4

Section 6 — Complete the Grid

On the left of each question below is a grid with one empty square.
Work out which of the five squares on the right should replace the empty square.

Example:

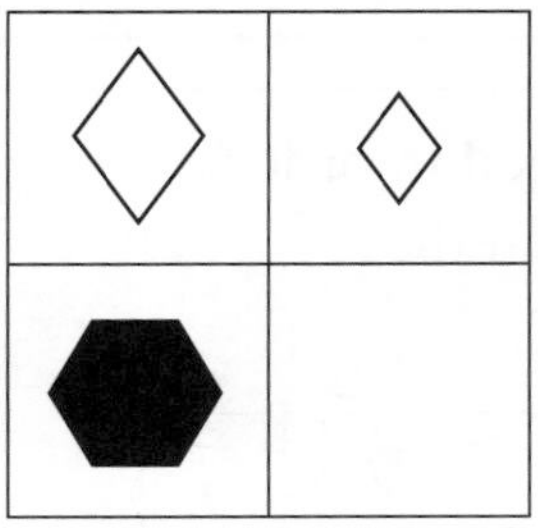

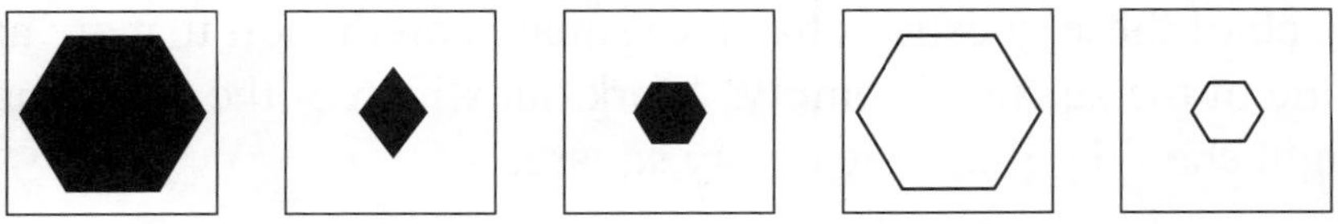

a b c d e

Answer: c

1

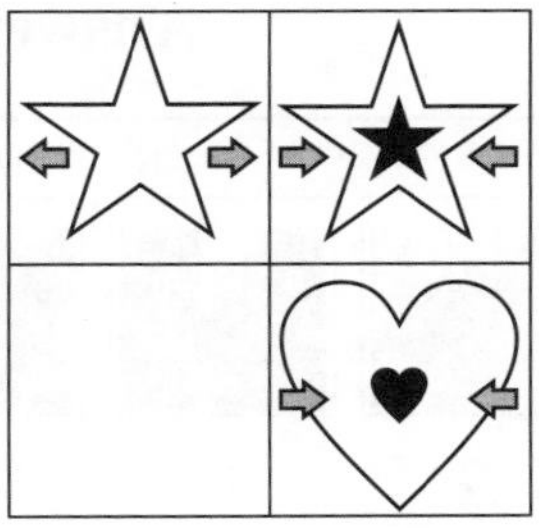

a b c d e

2

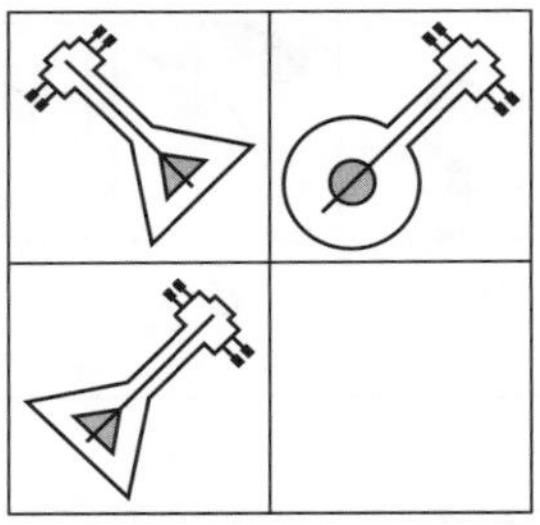

a b c d e

3

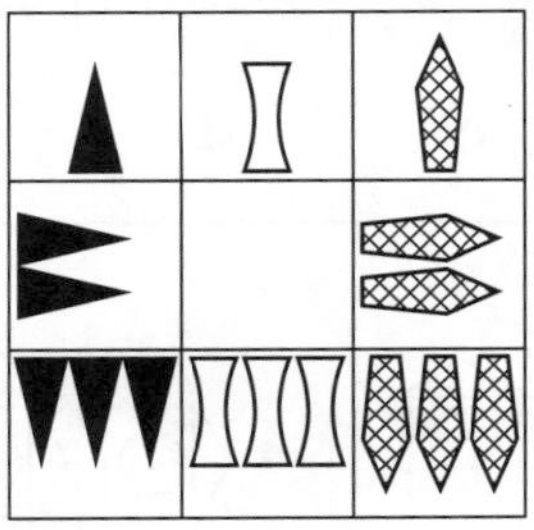

a b c d e

4

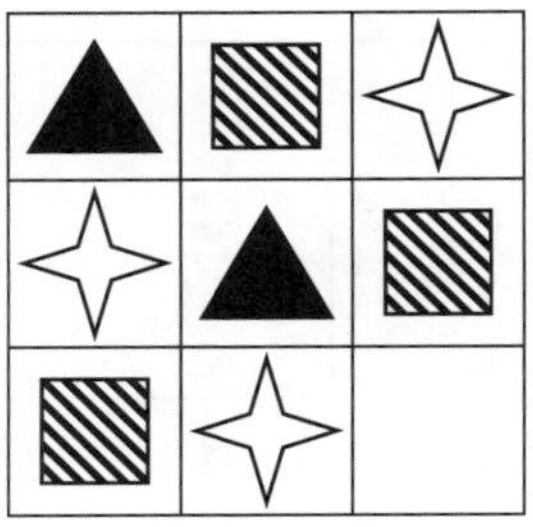

a b c d e

/ 4 Total / 28

END OF TEST

Assessment Test 10

You can print **multiple-choice answer sheets** for these questions from our website — go to www.cgplearning.co.uk/11+. If you'd prefer to answer them in standard write-in format, just circle the letter underneath your answer. The test should take around 15 minutes.

Section 1 — Complete the Series

Each of these questions has five squares on the left that are arranged in order. One of the squares is empty. Work out which of the five squares on the right should replace the empty square.

Example:

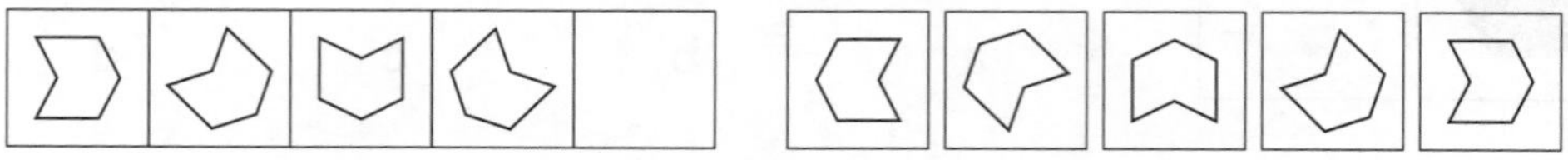

a b c d e

Answer: a

1

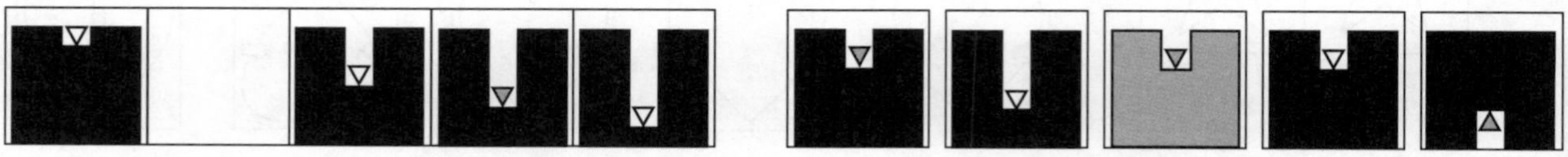

a b c d e

2

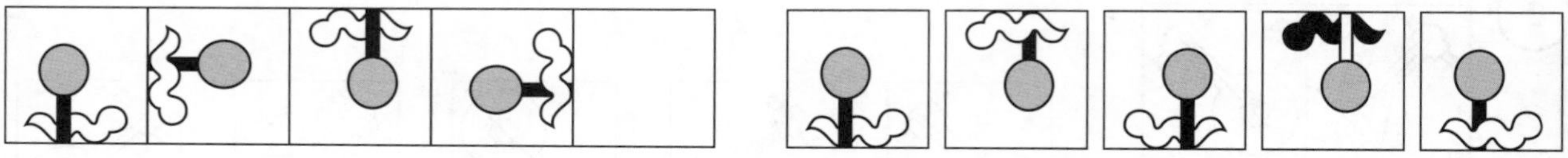

a b c d e

3

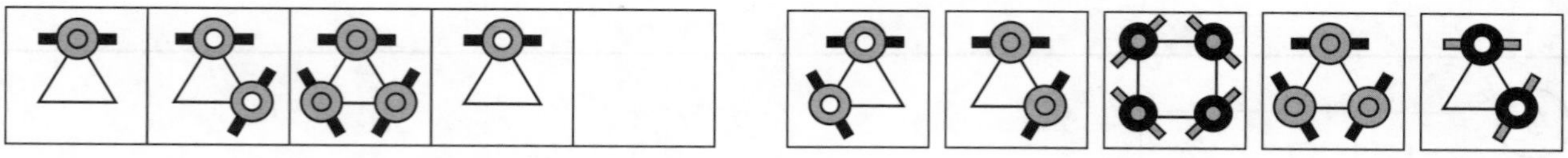

a b c d e

4

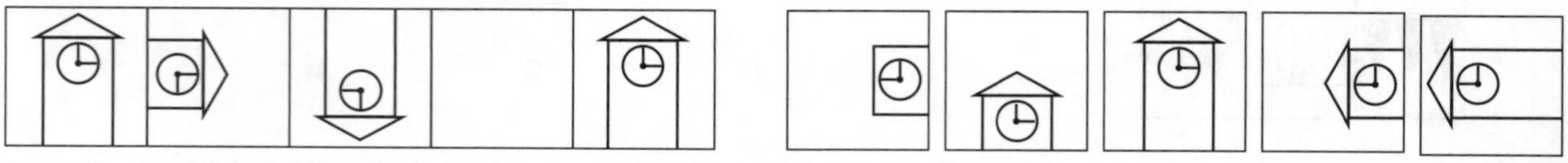

a b c d e

5

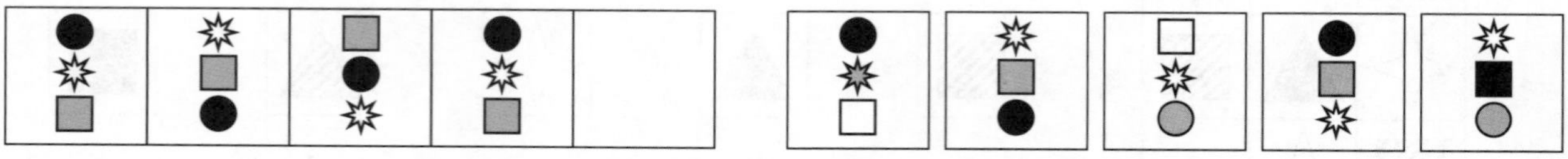

a b c d e

/ 5

Section 2 — Complete the Grid

On the left of each question below is a grid with one empty square.
Work out which of the five squares on the right should replace the empty square.

Example:

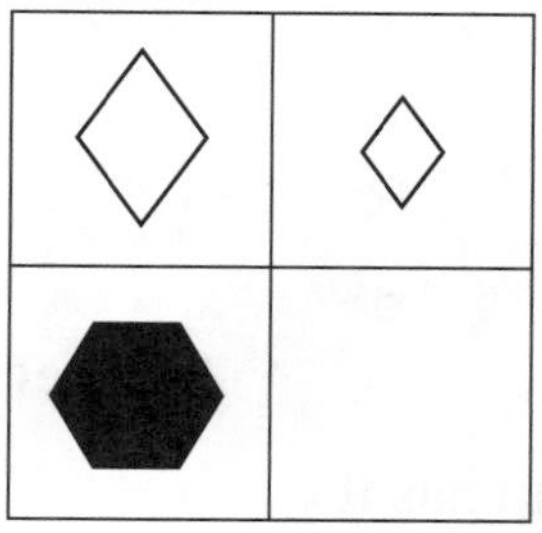

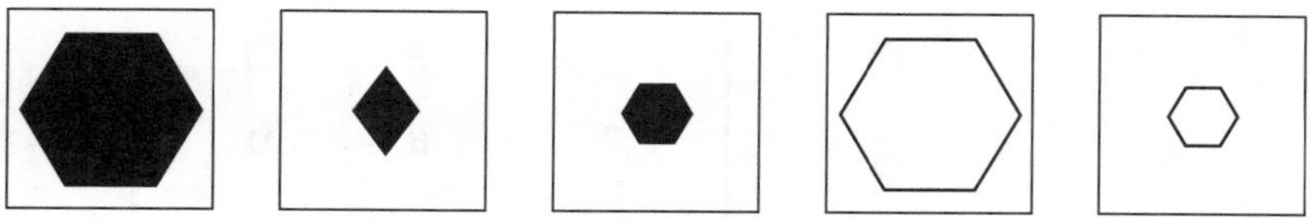

a b c d e

Answer: c

(1)

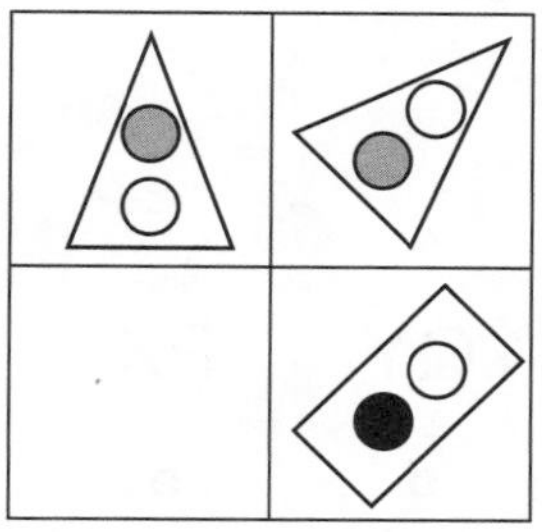

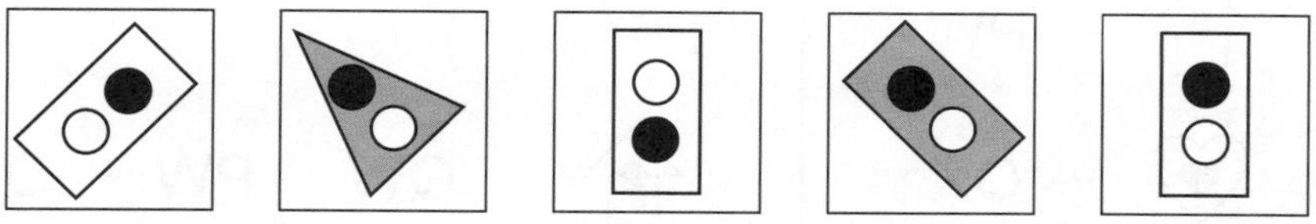

a b c d e

(2)

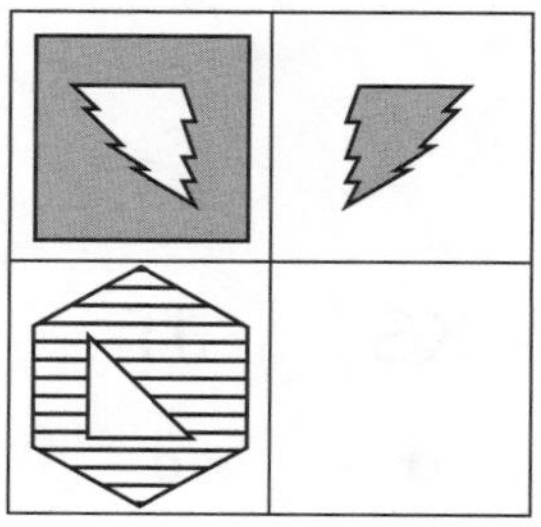

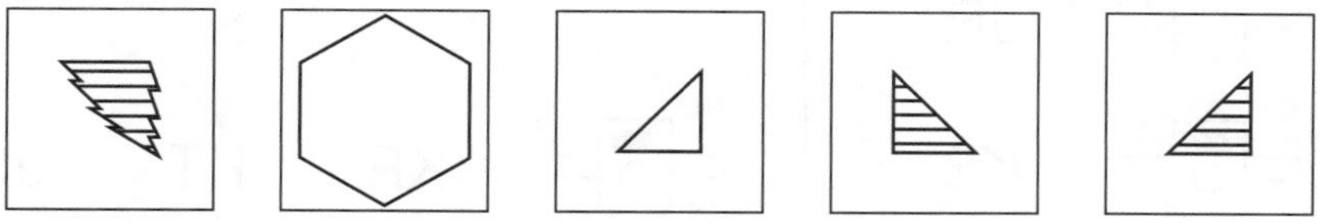

a b c d e

(3)

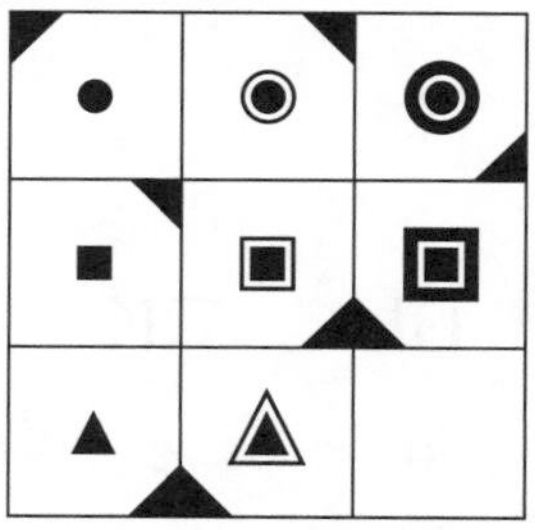

a b c d e

(4)

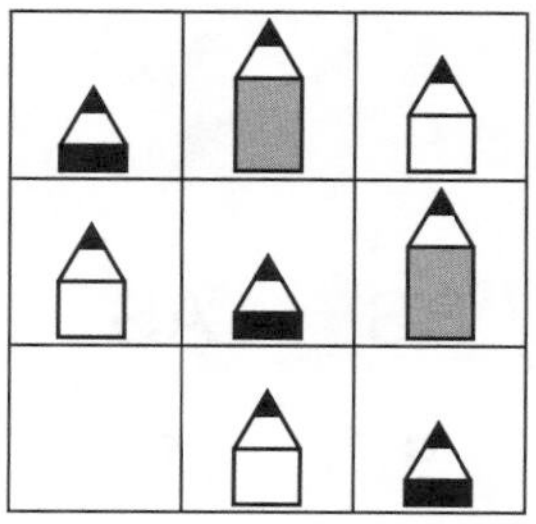

a b c d e

/ 4

Section 3 — Vertical Code

Each question has three figures on the left with code letters that describe them. You need to work out what the code letters mean. The figure on the right is missing its code. Work out which of the five codes on the right describes this figure.

Example:

 P

 Q

 R

P	Q	T	S	R
a	**b**	**c**	**d**	**e**

Answer: a

The arrow pointing right has the code letter P. The arrow pointing up has the code letter Q. The arrow pointing left has the code letter R. The figure on the right is an arrow pointing right, so its code must be P and the answer is **a**.

1

 PW

 QX

 PX

QW	PW	QX	QY	PX
a	**b**	**c**	**d**	**e**

2

 JR

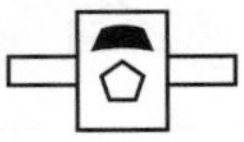 KS

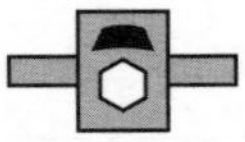 JT

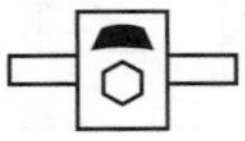

KR	KT	JS	KS	JT
a	**b**	**c**	**d**	**e**

3

 CK

 DL

 DK

CK	CM	CL	DL	DK
a	**b**	**c**	**d**	**e**

4

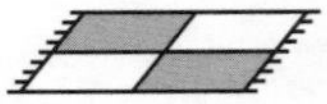 AS

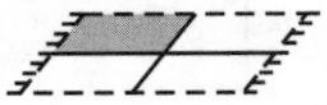 BR

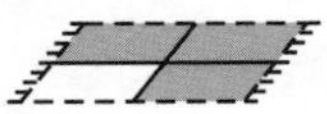 BT

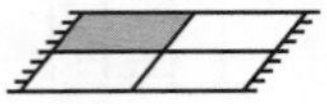

AT	AR	BT	BS	AS
a	**b**	**c**	**d**	**e**

/ 4

Section 4 — Find the Figure Like the First Three

In each question, there are three figures on the left that are like each other in some way. Work out which of the five figures on the right is most like the three figures on the left.

Example:

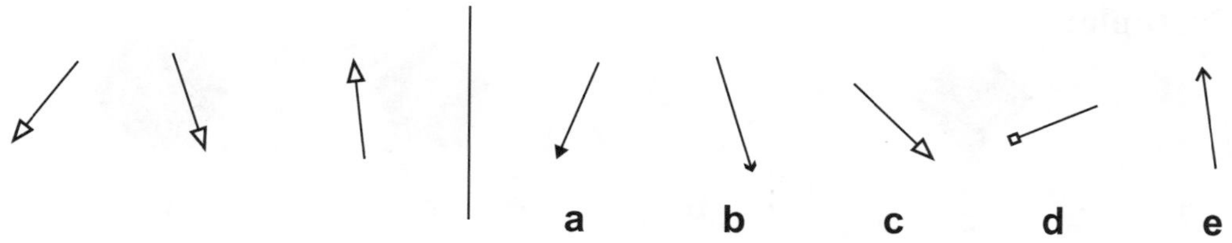

Answer: c

1

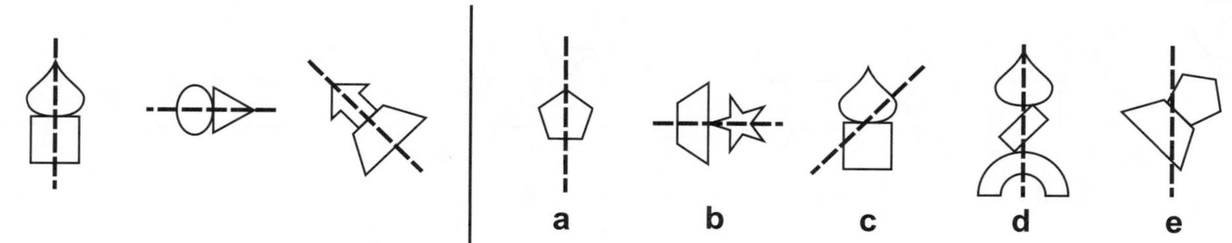

2

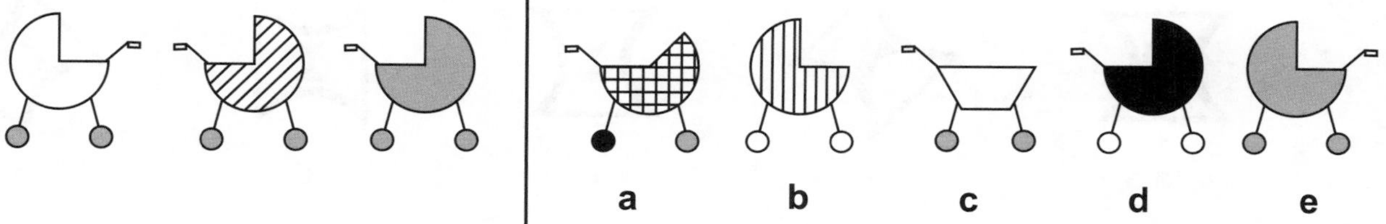

3

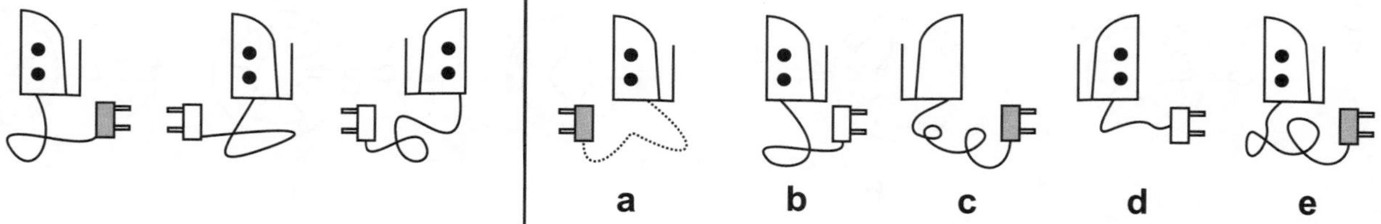

4

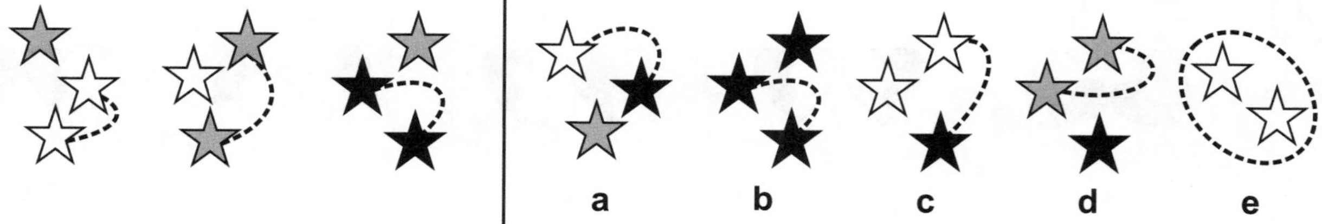

5

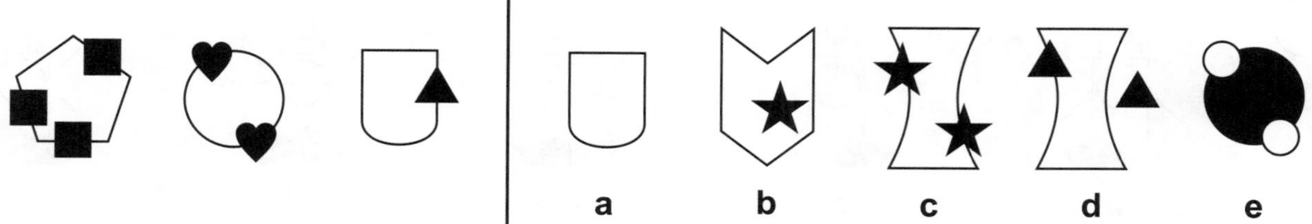

/ 5

Section 5 — Odd One Out

Each of the questions below has five figures.
Find the figure in each row that is most unlike the others.

Example:

a b c d e

Answer: b

1

a b c d e

2

a b c d e

3

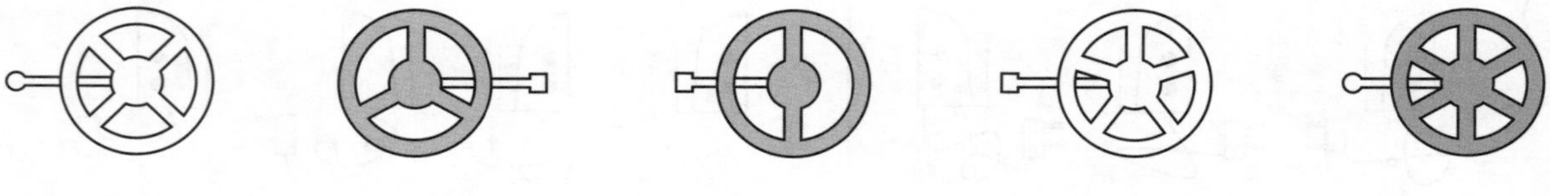

a b c d e

4

a b c d e

5

a b c d e

/ 5

Section 6 — Complete the Pair

The first figure in each question changes to become the second figure. Work out how the first figure has been changed. Then find the figure on the right that would match the third figure if it was changed in the same way.

Example:

a b c d e

Answer: e

1

a b c d e

2

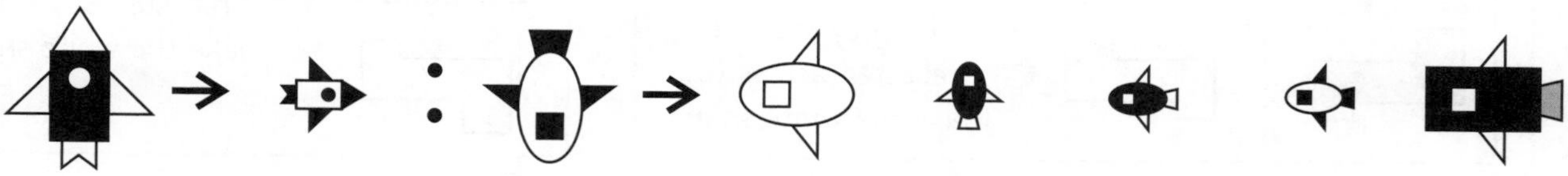

a b c d e

3

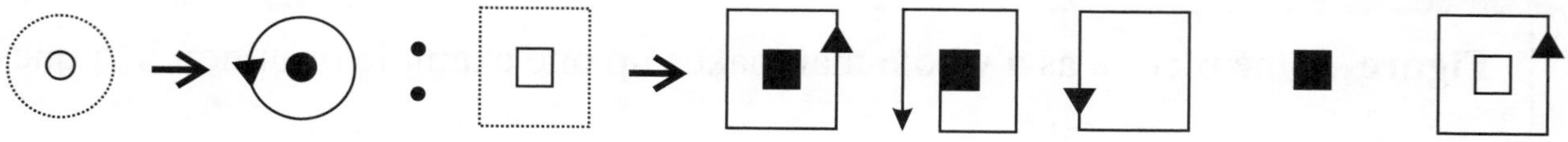

a b c d e

4

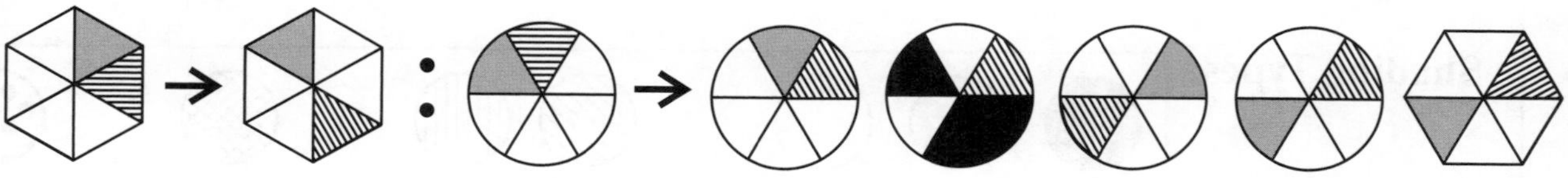

a b c d e

5

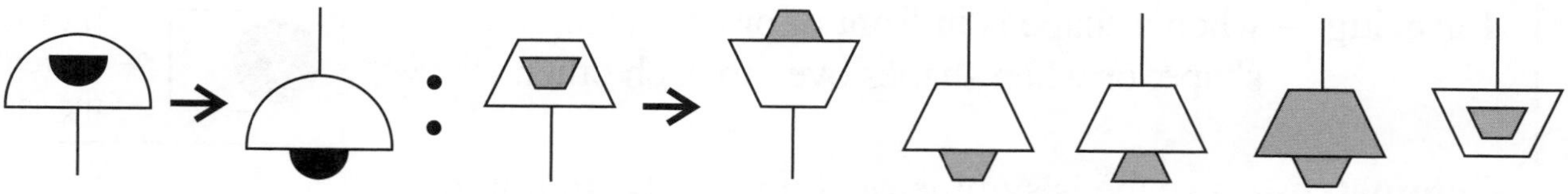

a b c d e

/ 5 Total / 28

Glossary

Rotation

Rotation is when a shape is **turned** clockwise or anticlockwise.

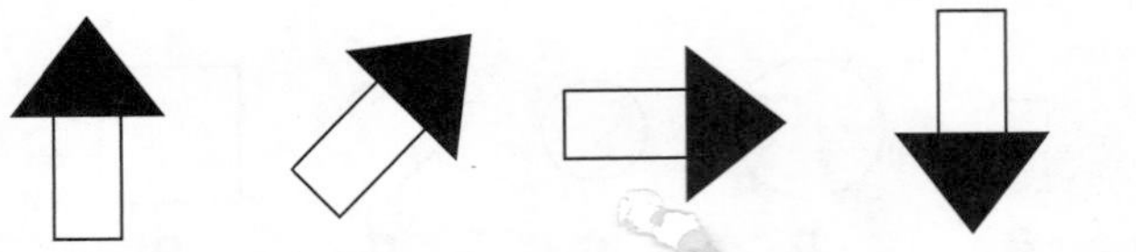

Example shape | 45 degree rotation | 90 degree rotation | 180 degree rotation

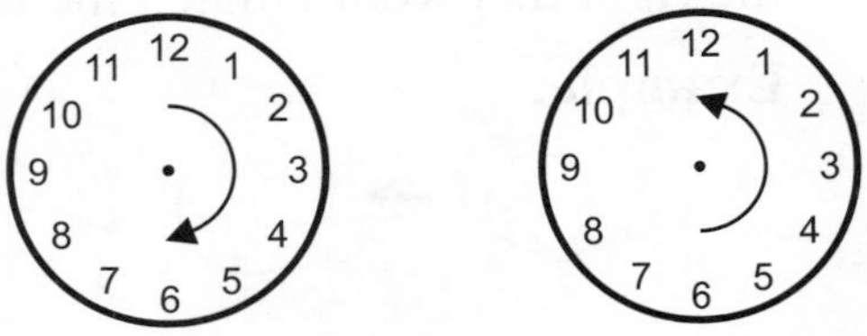

Clockwise is the direction that the hands on a clock move

Anticlockwise is the opposite direction

Reflection

Reflection is when something is **mirrored** over a line (this line might be invisible).

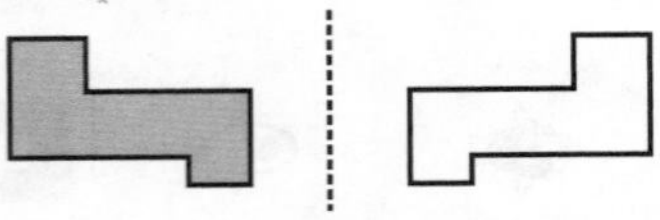

The grey shape is reflected across to make the white shape.

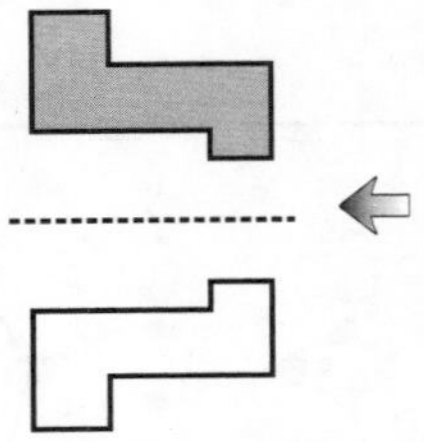

The grey shape is reflected down to make the white shape.

Other terms

Figure — the picture as a whole that makes up one example or option in a question.

Line Types:

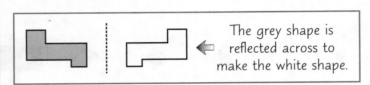

Thin | Thick | Dashed | Dotted | Curved | Jagged | Wavy

Shading Types:

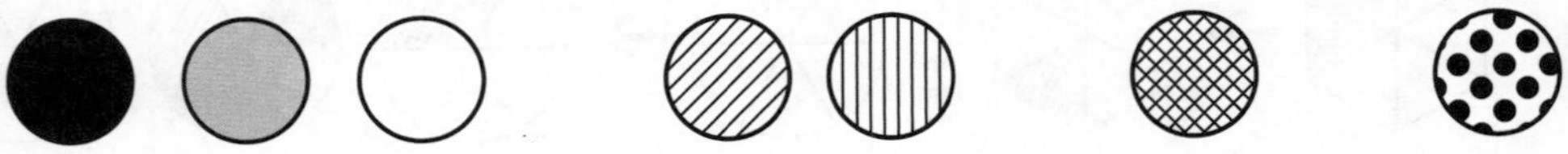

Black | Grey | White | Two types of hatching | Cross-hatched | Spotted

Layering — when a shape is in front of or behind another shape, or when shapes overlap each other.

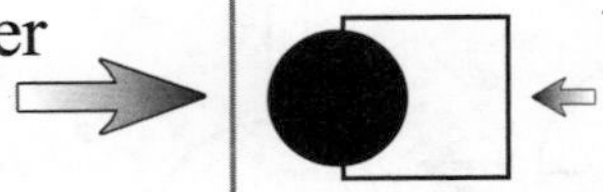

The circle is in front of the square.

Symmetry — a shape is symmetrical if it can be split into halves that are reflections of each other.